T0302598

Master of Zen: Extraordinary Teachings from Hui Neng's Altar Sutra

For those who are on the Bodhi path

Portions of Chapters 2-8 are adapted from Wong Mou-Lam's 1930 translation.

Library of Congress Cataloging-in-Publication Data

Huang, Tze-si, 1938-
Master of Zen : extraordinary teachings from Hui Neng's Altar sutra / translated and adapted by Tze-si Huang ; illustrated by Demi.
pages cm
Includes bibliographical references.
ISBN 978-1-936597-18-5 (pbk. : alk. paper) 1. Zen Buddhism. I. Demi, illustrator. II. Huineng, 638-713. Liuzu da shi fa bao tan jing. Adaptation of (work): III. Title.
BQ9265.6.H83 2012
294.3'927--dc23

2012009906

Printed in China on acid-free paper
For information address World Wisdom, Inc. P.O. Box 2682, Bloomington, Indiana 47402-2682
www.worldwisdom.com

Master of Zen

Extraordinary Teachings from Hui Neng's Altar Sutra

Translated and Adapted by
Tze-si Huang

Illustrated by
Demi

World Wisdom

Contents

Birth

In 638 A.D., in Shin-Gu County of Kwangtung Province, a little boy was born. At the time of his birth, miraculous lights and heavenly perfume filled his home.

The next morning, two monks suddenly appeared on his doorstep to congratulate the family and to offer a name.

They chose "Hui Neng."

Hui meaning: to apply the great *dharma* (universal law) in order to help all beings.

Neng meaning: the ability to spread Buddha's teaching to the world.

The two monks then disappeared as suddenly as they had come.

The parents adopted the name Hui Neng for their son, who would become the Sixth Patriarch of the Zen School.

The Diamond Sutra

Hui Neng's father died when he was three years old leaving him and his mother in great poverty. Growing up, Hui Neng collected firewood in the mountains and sold it in the marketplace. One day when Hui Neng was in the city, he heard a man reciting a *sutra*. As soon as he heard the words he became enlightened.

Hui Neng asked the man the name of the book he was reciting and was told that it was *The Diamond Sutra*. He further inquired where he came from and why he had recited this particular *sutra*. The man replied that he came from Tung Chan Monastery in the Huang Mei district of Ch'i Chou. The abbot in charge of the temple was Hung Jen, the Fifth Patriarch, and that there were about 1,000 disciples under him. He further told Hui Neng that His Holiness would encourage laity as well as the monks to recite this *sutra*, so they might realize their own essence of mind, and thereby reach Buddhahood directly.

Hui Neng was very happy and truly wanted to see the Fifth Patriarch. However he didn't have any money to support his mother. Probably due to good karma in past lives, Hui Neng was suddenly given ten taels of silver from a man who advised him to go immediately to Huang Mei to see the Fifth Patriarch.

After arrangements had been made for his mother, Hui Neng left for Huang Mei which took him more than a month to reach. Hui Neng went to pay homage to the Fifth Patriarch, and was asked where he came from and what he expected to get from him. Hui Neng replied, "I am a commoner from Hsin-Gu of Kwangtung. I have traveled far to pay you my respects and I ask for nothing but Buddhahood."

"You are a native of Kwangtung, a barbarian? How can you expect to be a Buddha?" asked the Fifth Patriarch. Hui Neng replied, "Although there are northern men and southern men, north and south makes no difference to their Buddha-nature. A barbarian may be different from Your Holiness physically, but there is no difference in his Buddha-nature."

The Fifth Patriarch was going to speak further to Hui Neng, but the presence of other disciples made him stop short.

"May I tell Your Holiness," said Hui Neng, "that Wisdom often rises in the mind. When one does not go astray from one's essence of mind, one may be called the 'field of merits.'"

The Fifth Patriarch thought, "This barbarian's much too bright!" So he told Hui Neng, "Go to the stable and do some work!" Hui Neng then went to the backyard where he was told by another monk to split firewood and pound rice.

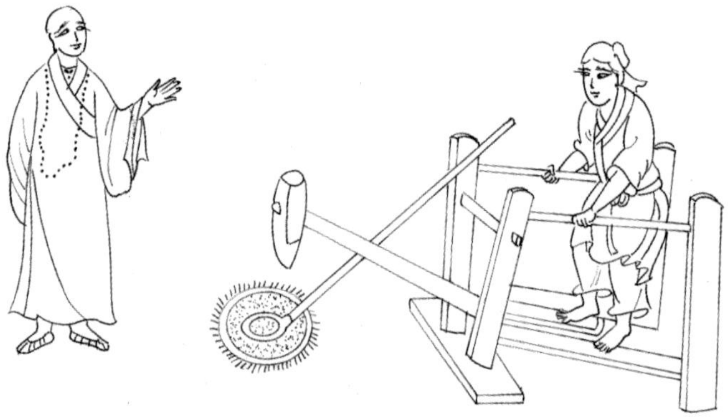

Splitting Firewood and Pounding Rice

Hui Neng quietly split firewood and pounded rice for more than eight months. One day the Fifth Patriarch came to see him and said, "I know your understanding of Buddhism is very sound, but I have to refrain from speaking to you lest evil doers should harm you. Do you understand?"

"Yes, Sir, I do," Hui Neng replied. "To avoid people taking notice of me, I dare not go near your hall."

The Fifth Patriarch Summons Disciples to Write a Stanza

The Fifth Patriarch one day assembled all his disciples and said to them, "The question of incessant rebirth is a momentous one. Day after day, instead of trying to free yourselves from this bitter sea of life and death, you seem to go after tainted merits only. Yet merits will be of no help, if your essence of mind is obscured. Go and seek Wisdom from your own mind and then write me a stanza about it. He who understands what the essence of mind is will be given the robe, the insignia of the patriarchate, and the *dharma*, and I shall make him the Sixth Patriarch. Go away quickly. Don't delay in writing your stanza. A deliberation is quite unnecessary and of no use. The man who has realized the essence of mind can easily speak of it at once, and cannot lose sight of it, even when engaged in battle."

Having received the instructions, the disciples said to one another, "The patriarchate will certainly be given to our instructor, Shen Hsiu. Therefore, there is no need for any of us to submit a stanza."

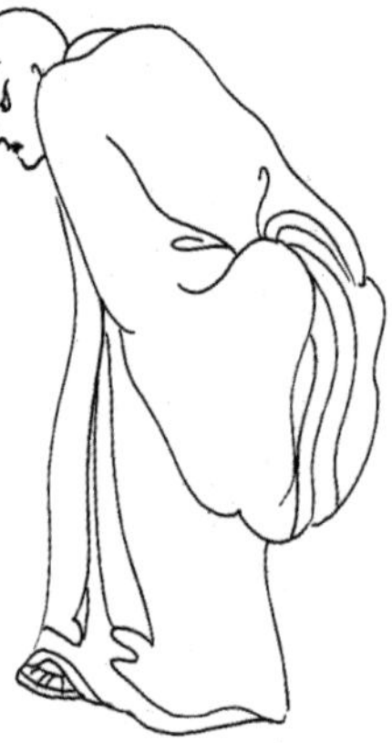

Shen Hsiu thought, "None of the disciples will submit a stanza for the patriarchate, since I am their instructor. I should submit a stanza to the patriarchate, otherwise the Patriarch will not know the level of my knowledge. If my object is for the *dharma*, it is good. If my motive is after the patriarchate, it is bad. Then my mind would be no different from the worldly: trying to rob the holy seat. If I do not submit a stanza, I would never have the chance to learn the *dharma*."

Having composed his stanza, Shen Hsiu tried several times to submit it to the Patriarch. However as soon as he went near the hall, he began to sweat profusely because he was so disturbed.

For four days he tried thirteen times and still failed to submit his stanza to the Fifth Patriarch. He thought to himself, "Instead of submitting my stanza directly to the Fifth Patriarch it would be better to write it on the corridor wall and let the Patriarch see it. If he thinks it's good, I'll come out to pay homage and tell him that it is my work. If he says it is bad, then I'll have wasted all these years meditating in this monastery and receiving deference which I do not deserve."

At the third watch of the night, Shen Hsiu, holding a lantern, wrote his stanza on the wall to express his vision. It read:

Our body is the *bodhi* (enlightenment) tree,
Our mind a mirror bright.
Carefully wipe them by the hour,
So no dust will alight.

Shen Hsiu Did Not Know the Essence of Mind

Shen Hsiu returned to his room right after writing his stanza. He again thought, "If the Patriarch sees my stanza tomorrow and approves it, it means that I am ready for the *dharma*. If he considers it badly done, it would mean that I am not qualified for the *dharma* due to sins in my previous lives which clouded my mind." He kept on thinking in this way and was not able to sit or sleep in peace.

The Patriarch already knew that Shen Hsiu had not attained enlightenment, nor seen his own self-nature (*tsi-hsin*).

In the morning the Patriarch sent for his artist who was going to paint Buddhas on the walls. Suddenly he saw Shen Hsiu's stanza. He told the artist, "There is no need to paint now. As the *sutra* says, "All forms are temporary and illusive. Just leave the stanza on the wall so that people who practice it accordingly can save themselves from falling into evil realms of existence and gain great merits."

He ordered his disciples to burn incense and express respect for the stanza and told all his disciples to pay homage to the stanza and recite it, so that they might see their essence of mind. All the disciples recited it, and all exclaimed, "It is great."

At the third watch of the night, the Patriarch summoned Shen Hsiu to the hall and asked whether the stanza was written by him. Shen Hsiu replied, "It was. I do not dare to get the patriarchate. I just wish your holiness would kindly tell me whether I have a little bit of wisdom?" The Patriarch said: "Your stanza shows that you have not seen your own self-nature. You have reached the door of enlightenment, but you have not entered it yet. To attain supreme enlightenment one must spontaneously be able to know one's own self-nature which is neither created nor destroyed. You must go back to think it over for a couple of days and submit another stanza. If your stanza shows that you have entered the door, I'll transmit the *dharma* and the robe to you."

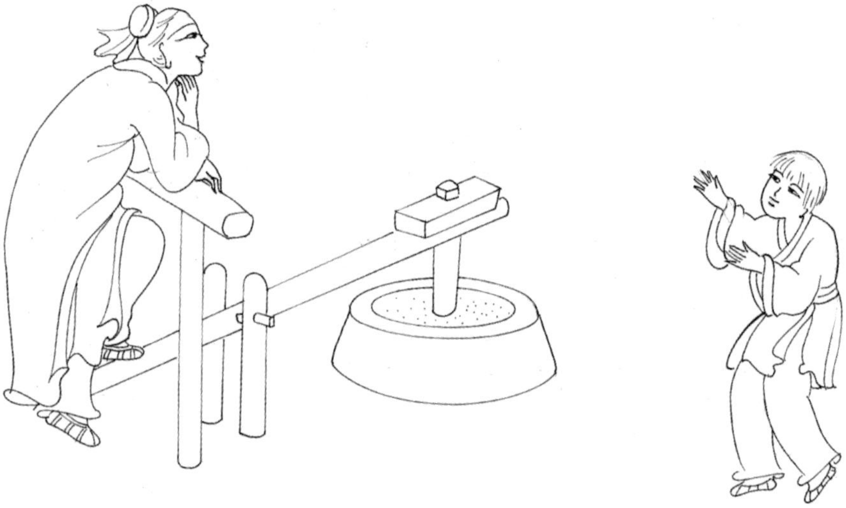

For several days Shen Hsiu was in a state of confusion and disturbance and unable to write another stanza. Two days later a young boy passed by the room where Hui Neng was pounding rice. He was reciting Shen Hsiu's stanza. After hearing it, Hui Neng immediately knew that the writer of the stanza had not seen his essence of mind. Hui Neng asked, "What stanza is this?" The boy said, "You barbarian! The Patriarch has told his disciples that life and death is a serious matter. Those who want to inherit the *dharma* and the robe should submit a stanza, and if one understands the essence of mind, he'll transmit the *dharma* and the robe to him."

The boy said, "Instructor Shen Hsiu wrote this 'formless' stanza on the corridor wall and the Fifth Patriarch told all of us to recite it." Hui Neng told the boy that he also wanted to recite the stanza and asked the boy to show him where the stanza was so that he could bow before it.

Then the boy took Hui Neng to see the stanza. At that time a local official happened to be there. Hui Neng said to the official, "As I am illiterate, will you kindly read the stanza for me?" After the stanza was read, Hui Neng said that he also had a stanza, and asked the official to write it on the wall for him. The official said, "Barbarian! What a strange thing! You can compose a stanza?"

Hui Neng said: "If you are a true seeker of enlightenment do not despise a beginner. The people of the lowest class may have the highest intelligence; the people of the highest class may not have much intelligence. To insult others is a serious sin." The official said, "Tell me your stanza. I will write it down for you, but don't forget to deliver me first if you receive the *dharma*."

Hui Neng's stanza read:

There is no *bodhi* tree,
Nor stand of mirror bright.
Since everything is emptiness,
Where can dust alight?

Great Surprise

When Hui Neng's stanza had been written, all the disciples were very surprised. They expressed great admiration for him, and said to one another, "It is truly unbelievable; we should not judge others by their appearances."

The Fifth Patriarch seeing that the crowd was overcome with surprise and amazement, and fearful that someone might do harm to Hui Neng, rubbed off the stanza with his shoe. Then he said to the crowd that the writer of the stanza had not yet realized the essence of mind.

Supreme Enlightenment

Next day the Fifth Patriarch went to the room where Hui Neng was pounding rice with a stone pestle. The Fifth Patriarch said, "A seeker of the way risks his life for the *dharma*. Should he do so?" Then he asked, "Is the rice ready?"

Hui Neng replied, "The rice was ready a long time ago, only waiting for the sieve." The Fifth Patriarch hit the mortar three times with his cane and left.

Hui Neng got the subtle message. At the third watch of the night, he went to the room of the Fifth Patriarch, who covered the window with a robe so that no one could see inside. Then the Fifth Patriarch expounded *The Diamond Sutra* for him. When he came to the sentence, "One should use one's mind without attachment," Hui Neng immediately attained complete enlightenment and realized that all things in the universe are not separate from the essence of mind.

Transmission

Hui Neng said to the Fifth Patriarch, "Who would have known that the essence of mind is originally pure; who would have known that the essence of mind is free from birth and death; who would have known that the essence of mind is intrinsically self-sufficient; who would have known that all things are manifested from the essence of mind?"

Knowing Hui Neng had realized his original nature, the Fifth Patriarch said, "One who has realized his original nature is called a great man, teacher of heavenly and sentient beings, and a Buddha."

Thus, Hui Neng was given the *dharma* at midnight, unknown to anyone. The *dharma* of Immediacy was transmitted to him and he was given the bowl and robe.

The Fifth Patriarch said, "Now you are the Sixth Patriarch. Carefully preserve the *dharma* and do not let it die out, and deliver all beings everywhere. Listen to my verse:

Sow the seeds of enlightenment
And reap the fruits of Buddhahood.
Let nature take its formless course
Without effort you are there."

Self-Salvation

The Fifth Patriarch continued, "When the great master Bodhidharma came to this land, people did not believe him. So he handed on the robe and the bowl as the concrete symbol of faith. It has been inherited through many generations. As for the *dharma*, it is transmitted from heart to heart (mind to mind) and to be self-realized. Since the robe is the focus of contention, it stops with you and is not to be handed on anymore. If you continue to pass on the robe, your life may be in danger. Now you should leave here immediately, otherwise someone may harm you."

Hui Neng asked, "Where should I go?" The Fifth Patriarch replied, "Stop at Huai, hide at Hui."

Hui Neng said, "I am a southerner and do not know the way." The Fifth Patriarch said, "Don't worry, I'll take you there."

So the Fifth Patriarch took Hui Neng to Chiu-chiang where they boarded a boat. The Fifth Patriarch took up the oars and started to row. Hui Neng said, "Please sit down, let your disciple row."

The Fifth Patriarch said, "It is appropriate that I ferry you across." Hui Neng said:

"When the disciple is at a loss,
The teacher ferries him over.
When the disciple is enlightened,
He ferries himself across."

The Fifth Patriarch said, "It is so, it is so." The Fifth Patriarch continued, "From now on Buddhist *dharma* will be spread widely through you. Three years from now I'll depart from this world. Now you should go to the south but do not start promoting the *dharma* too soon. It is a difficult task."

After he bade farewell to the Fifth Patriarch, Hui Neng headed south. He came to Mount Ta Yu two months later.

Disciples Surprised

The Fifth Patriarch returned to the monastery and for several days he did not show up to lecture. The disciples were bewildered, and inquired whether the Fifth Patriarch was sick. The Fifth Patriarch replied, "I am not sick. The *dharma* and the robe have gone south." The disciples asked, "Who has received the transmission?" The Fifth Patriarch said, "The capable one got it." Then the disciples knew who was the one, because the word "capable" was the meaning of *neng*, as in Hui Neng.

Immediately several hundred monks started to chase Hui Neng, trying to take the robe and the bowl from him. Among them there was a rough monk named Hui-Ming who found Hui Neng first in the mountains. Hui Neng put the robe and the bowl on a rock and hid himself in the bush. Hui-Ming saw the robe and the bowl and tried to take them, but he was not able to move them. Then he called out, "Brother, I came here for the *dharma*, not for the robe."

Hui Neng came out from the bush and sat on the rock. Hui-Ming bowed and said, "Brother, please teach me the *dharma*." Hui Neng said, "Since you came for the *dharma*, I'll explain it to you. But first you must clear your mind and get rid of all thoughts."

Hui-Ming sat silently for a long time, then Hui Neng told Hui-Ming, "When you do not think of good, and do not think of bad, what is your original face?" At these words, Hui-Ming was enlightened at once. Then he asked, "In addition to what you just said, do you have any more secrets?"

Hui Neng said, "What I have told you is no secret. If you reflect inwardly you'll find the secret is inside of you."

Hui-Ming said, "Although I practiced hard at Huang Mei, I did not really see my essence of mind. Now after receiving your instruction, I feel I am just like a person who takes a drink of water and knows for himself whether it is warm or cold. Now you are my teacher." Then he asked, "Where should I go?"

Hui Neng said, "Stop at Yuen. Stay at Meng." Hui-Ming bowed and took leave. Hui-Ming came down the mountain. He told the group of pursuers that he had searched everywhere but there was no trace of Hui Neng. He suggested that they should go elsewhere to find him.

Later when Hui Neng came to Ts'uo-Chi, he again was chased by evil people. He took refuge among a group of hunters in Ssu-Ming Range. He stayed there for fifteen years. Occasionally he explained the *dharma* to them as the opportunity arose.

A Mind Moving Surprise

One day Hui Neng realized the time had come to spread the *dharma*. He left the hunters and went west to the Fa-hsin temple in Kwangtung Province. There Master Yin-Tsung was expounding *The Nirvana Sutra*.

At that time there was a wind blowing and the banners were flapping. Two monks were arguing: One monk said, "The wind is moving." Another monk said, "The banners are moving."

They kept on arguing until Hui Neng came forward and said, "It is not the wind that is moving. It is not the banners that are moving. It is your mind that is moving." The monks were very surprised. Master Yin-Tsung invited Hui Neng to the high seat and inquired about the profound meaning of Buddhism.

Master Yin-Tsung was deeply impressed by his answers which were accurate, original, concise and to the point, clearly not from book learning. Master Yin-Tsung said, "Definitely you are not an ordinary person. For a long time I have heard that the *dharma* of Huang Mei and the robe had come south. Are you the one?"

Hui Neng said, "I do not dare to assume." Master Yin-Tsung bowed and asked Hui Neng to show the robe and bowl to the community. Master Yin-Tsung asked, "What is the process of *dharma* transmission in Huang Mei?" Hui Neng said, "There was no particular process for transmission. The only concern was seeing the essential self-nature. It was not a matter of meditation or liberation."

Master Yin-Tsung said, "Why is it not a matter of meditation or liberation?"

Hui Neng answered, "Buddhist teaching is non-dualistic. Meditation and liberation are two things, hence they are not Buddhism."

Master Yin-Tsung asked, "What is non-dualistic Buddhism?" Hui Neng replied, "You have just expounded *The Nirvana Sutra*. It clearly explains that Buddhism is a non-dualistic teaching. For example, the *bodhisattva* King Kuei-Te asked Buddha, 'Those who have violated the four serious prohibitions and committed the five perverse sins, would they be cut off from the roots of goodness and the essential nature (*tsi-hsin*) of Buddhahood?' Buddha replied, 'Roots of goodness are twofold: One is permanent, one is impermanent. Buddha-nature is neither permanent nor impermanent. Therefore the roots of goodness are not cut off.' That is non-duality. Furthermore, one is good, one is bad. Buddha-nature is neither good nor bad. This is called non-duality. Ordinary people consider their bodies and the world as two. People who are awakened realize that the essential nature is one."

Having heard these expositions, Master Yin-Tsung joyfully joined his palms together and said, "My lectures on the *sutras* are like gravel: your discourse is like pure gold." Master Yin-Tsung regarded Hui Neng as his teacher.

After he attained supreme enlightenment, for many years, Hui Neng experienced extreme hardship and danger, as if his life were hanging by a thread. Finally, Hui Neng was able to open up Tung-shan school and started to preach non-dualistic Buddhism.

He told the assembly, "The teaching of immediacy was transmitted by past sages; it is not my personal wisdom. Those who wish to learn the teaching should first of all clear their minds, and eliminate all doubts afterwards. Then you will be no different from sages of the past."

Return to Chao-Chi

Later that year, Master Yin-Tsung conducted the head shaving ceremony for the Sixth Patriarch. He wanted to return to Chao-Chi Bo-ling Temple. A group of more than 1,000 people escorted him all the way back to Chao-Chi. Also, several hundred people including monks, scholars, and laymen took refuge with the Sixth Patriarch.

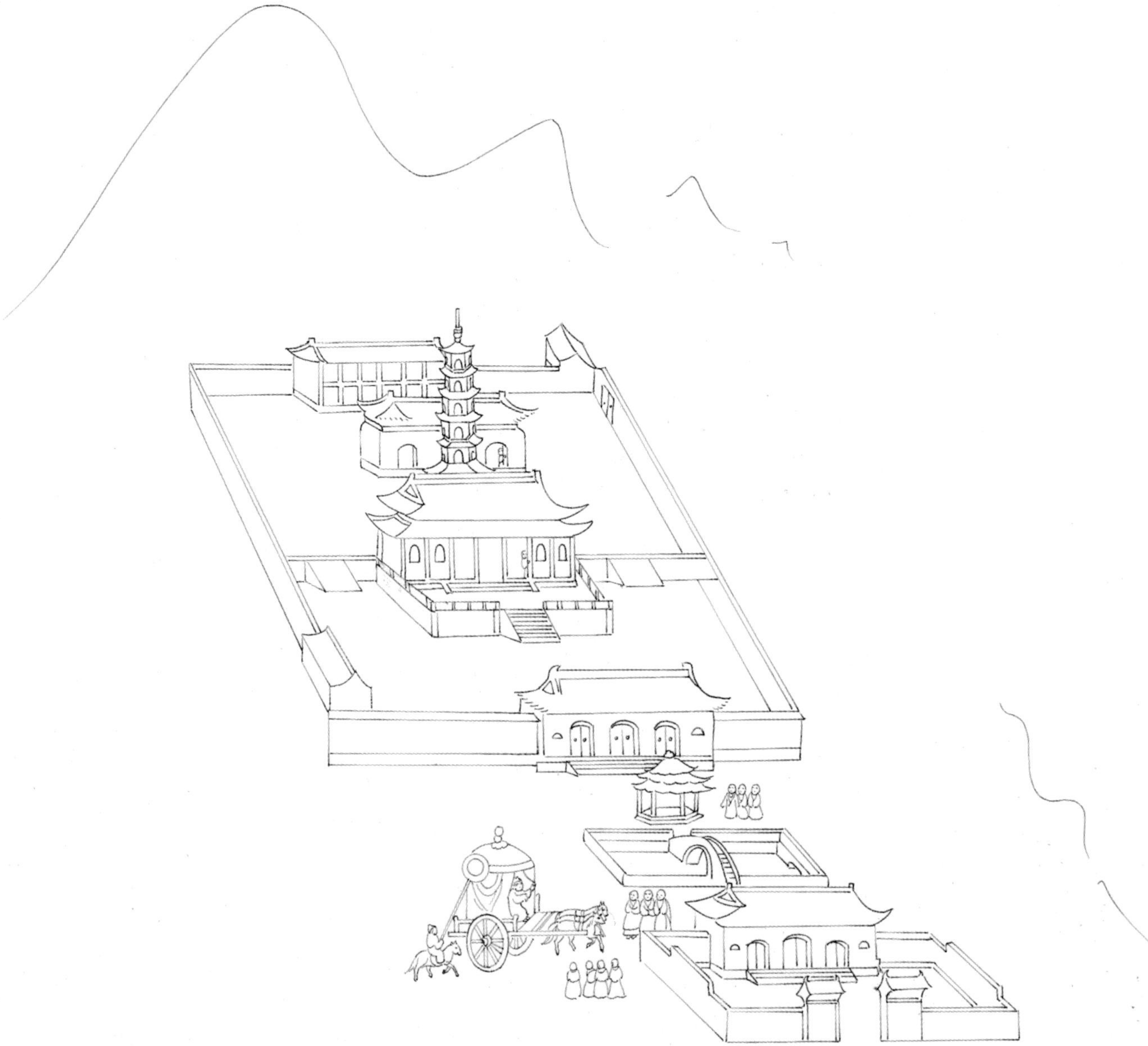

The Lion's Roar

The Sixth Patriarch became very well known shortly after he opened up the school in Bo-lin Temple. It quickly became the learning center of the *Ch'an* (*Zen*) teaching. Governor Wei of Chao-Chi was a devoted Buddhist. Joined by many friends and colleagues they came to Bo-lin Temple to invite the Sixth Patriarch to the Ta-fen Temple in the city of Chu-Chiang to lecture on the *dharma*.

The next day the Sixth Patriarch took the high chair and said to the assembly of more than 1,000 people: "Good friends, people of the world originally have the wisdom of *bodhi* and *prajna* within themselves. The reason they cannot realize it is because their mind is clouded and confused. Therefore, they need an enlightened teacher to explain it to them and guide them so they can recognize their essential nature.

"In the Buddha-nature, there is basically no difference between wise and ignorant people. The real difference is that one group is clouded and confused while the other is enlightened.

"Now I will explain to you the *dharma* of *maha-prajnaparamita*, so that you may gain wisdom. Listen attentively with a focused mind.

"People of the world who recite the word *prajna* all day long without recognizing that the *prajna* is within their essential nature are like people talking about food without eating. People who only talk about emptiness will never find their essential nature. It has no benefit.

"*Maha-prajnaparamita* is a Sanskrit word. It means the 'great wisdom has reached the other shore.' This must be practiced mentally, not just by verbal recitation. Verbal recitation without mental effort is like dew and lightning. It is illusory and disappears quickly. When it is practiced both verbally and mentally, then the mind and speech correspond.

"The original essential nature is Buddha. Apart from it there is no Buddha to be found.

"What does *maha* mean? *Maha* means great. The expanse of the mind is as vast as space without bounds. It has no head or tail. It has no squareness, no roundness, no largeness or smallness; it has no blueness, yellowness, redness, or whiteness. It has no up or down, long or short; it has no anger or joy; no right or wrong, no good or bad; no head or tail.

"All the Buddha lands are like that. People's original self-nature is also like that.

"Deluded people talk, wise people act. There are people who think that by sitting quietly with an empty mind without any thought is great. This is a wrong view.

"Don't ever fixate on emptiness. If you sit quietly with emptiness in mind, you may fall into the deep void of indifference.

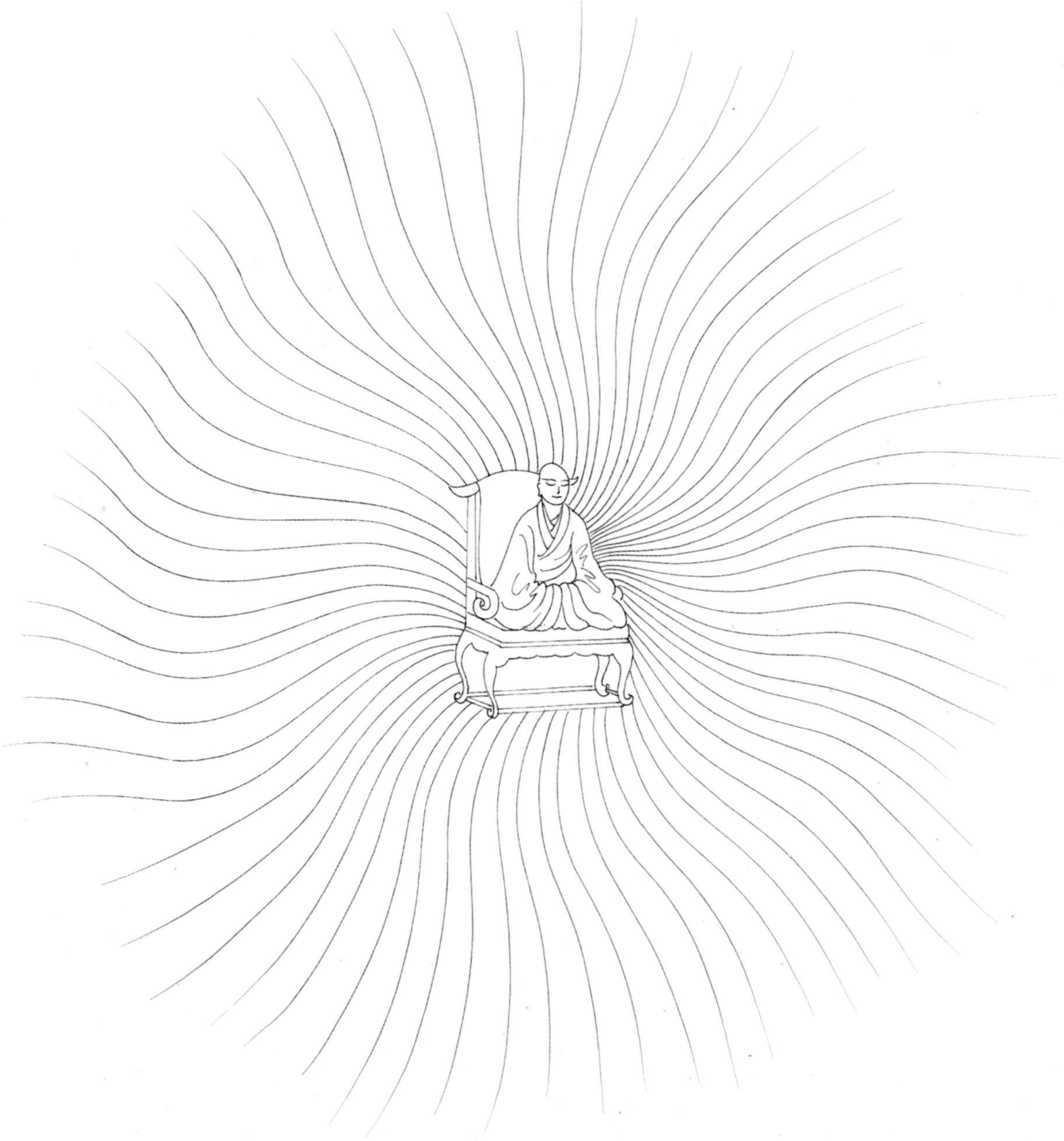

"The empty space of the universe contains the colors and forms of all things: the sun, moon, stars, mountains, rivers, land, springs, streams, grasses, trees, forests, good people, bad people, good things, bad things, heavens, hells, oceans, etc. They are all within 'empty' space. The emptiness of people's essential nature is also like that. It contains everything. It is great—*maha*.

"Hence, one is everything, everything is one, coming and going freely without mental blockage. This is *prajna*.

"*Paramita* means reaching the other shore liberated.

"*Maha-prajnaparamita* is most magnificent, illuminating, and without equal."

Virtues and Blessings

In another assembly, Governor Wei said he had heard the story of Grand Master Bodhidharma's first meeting with Emperor Wu of Liang. The Emperor asked, "All my life I have been building temples, supporting monks, giving alms, and charity meals. How much merit and virtue have I achieved?" Grand Master Bodhidharma replied, "In fact, no merit and no virtue have been achieved." The Governor asked the Sixth Patriarch to explain why?

The Sixth Patriarch said: "It is true, there is no merit and virtue in building temples, etc. Do not doubt the words of the ancient sages. The mind of the Emperor was incorrect. He did not understand the true meaning of the *dharma*. The activities of building temples, etc. is called 'seeking blessings.' Merits and virtues are in the *dharma* body, not in the cultivation of blessings."

The Sixth Patriarch continued: "Seeing the essential nature is merit, equanimity is virtue. Without stagnation from thought to thought, constantly seeing the true subtle function of essential nature is merit and virtue. Inward humility is merit, outward respect is virtue. The self essential nature establishing all *dharmas* (things) is merit. The mind detached from thoughts is virtue. Not detaching from self essential nature is virtue. Acting without defilement is virtue.

"Good friends, merit and virtue must be seen within the self essential nature and not be sought through giving and offering. Emperor Wu did not know the principle of *dharma*. Grand Master Bodhidharma was not in error."

The Western Pure Land

Governor Wei said: "I often see monks and laity reciting 'Amitabha Buddha' and vowing to be reborn in the Western Pure Land. Would you tell us whether they can be reborn in the Pure Land?"

The Sixth Patriarch replied: "Listen clearly, I'll explain it to you: When the World-Honored One (Shakyamuni Buddha) was in the city of Sravasti, expounding the *sutra* he said that according to the *sutra*, it was very clear that the Pure Land is not far from here. Treatises suggested that it is 108,000 miles away. This number refers to the ten evils and eight perversions in one's mind. For the people of less capacity it is far away. For the people with great capacity is it near.

"There are two kinds of people, the wise and the dull, but the truth is not two. It differs between delusion and enlightenment, between quick and slow. Deluded people invoke Amitabha Buddha, seeking to be reborn in the Pure Land, while enlightened ones purify their own minds. That's why Buddha said, 'When your mind is pure the Buddha land is pure accordingly.'"

The Sixth Patriarch continued, "Now I urge you to get rid of the ten evils; that is equivalent to crossing 100,000 miles. Then do away with the eight perversions, that is equivalent to 8,000 miles. See the essential nature in every thought, always act with equality and directness, then in an instant you will see Amitabha Buddha."

The Sixth Patriarch asked, "Would you like to see the Western Pure Land this instant?" The crowd bowed and said, "We wish the Patriarch would be so compassionate as to cause the Western Pure Land to appear before us!"

The Sixth Patriarch said: "The physical body of a human being is a city. There are six gates: the outer gates are the eyes, ears, nose, tongue, body, and the one inner gate is the gate of consciousness. The mind is the ground, nature is the king. The king lives on the ground of the mind. When the essential nature is there, the king is there; when the essential nature is not there, the king disappears. When the essential nature is there, both body and mind exist. When the essential nature is gone, the body disintegrates.

"Buddhahood is realized within the essential nature. Do not seek it outside. If your own nature is confused, you are an ordinary person; if your own nature is enlightened, you are a Buddha.

"Kindness and compassion are Avalokitesvara; joyfulness and giving are Mahasthamaprapta; stillness and purity are Shakyamuni; equanimity and directness are Amitabha. Distinction of self from others is Mount Sumeru's blockade; greed and the crooked mind are the rip tides of the oceans; afflictions are tsunami waves; viciousness and cruelty are the violent dragons; falsehoods and delusions are ghosts and evil spirits; worldly passions are the poisonous fish and turtles; greed and anger are the hells, and stupidities are the lowly animals.

"Always practice the ten virtues and heaven will appear before you. Get rid of distinctions of self from others and Mount Sumeru's blockade will open. Eliminate greed and the crooked mind and the rip tides will cease; without afflictions the waves will be still. Do away with viciousness and cruelty and the dragons and poisonous fish will disappear. On the ground of your mind, the enlightened nature of the *tathagata* (the realized one) radiates abundant light, outwardly illuminating the six gates, enough to penetrate the heavens, and inwardly illuminating your own essential nature. Then the three poisons of greed, anger, and ignorance are eliminated, and all signs of the hells disappear at once. When inside and outside are completely illuminated you are no different from those born in the Western Pure Land."

Hearing this explanation, the assembly clearly saw the essential nature. They all bowed and praised the Sixth Patriarch chanting, "Excellent, may all living beings in the universe awaken and immediately understand this wonderful *dharma*."

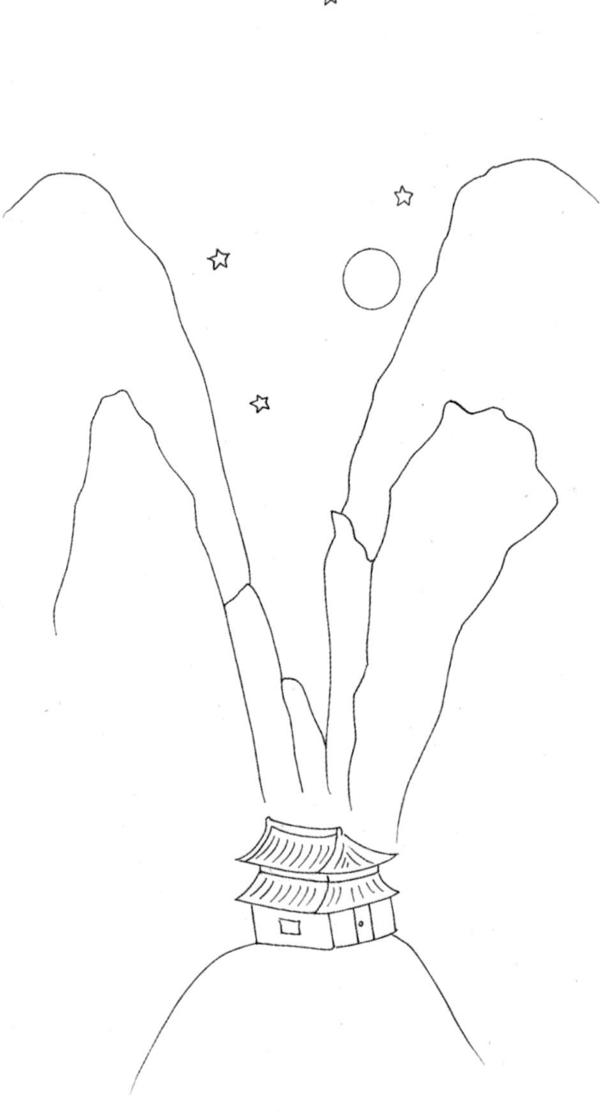

The Formless Hymn

Governor Wei asked: "As laity, how do we practice? Please give us instructions."

The Sixth Patriarch replied: "If you want to put this into practice, you can do it at home, it does not have to be in a monastery. As long as your mind is clear, regardless of where you practice, laity or clergy, it is good."

The Sixth Patriarch added: "Now I'll compose a 'formless hymn' for you. As long as you practice in accordance with it you'll always be with me. If you do not practice in accordance with it, there will be no benefit from shaving your head and leaving home.

When the mind sees things evenly, there's no need for precepts.
When action is straightforward, there's no need for *Ch'an*.
If you are filial, you'll take care of your parents;
If you are dutiful, above and below are in accord.

If you are considerate, high and low are harmonious.
If you are tolerant, no evil can disturb you.
If you can drill wood and produce fire
Red lotus flowers will rise from the mud.

True words are good medicine;
Honest speech can offend the ear.
Correct your errors and develop wisdom;
Hiding shortcomings reveals the petty mind.

Enlightenment can only be found in the mind:
Why seek mysteries from outside?
Hear these words and practice accordingly,
And the Western Pure Land will appear before you!"

The Sixth Patriarch added, "All of you should put this hymn into practice. See your essential nature, and reach Buddhahood directly."

The Lamp of Stabilization, Stillness, and Insight

The Sixth Patriarch said: "My teaching is based on stabilization and insightful wisdom. Don't be confused and think that stabilization and insightful wisdom are separate. They are one, not two. Stabilization is the substance of insightful wisdom, which is the application of stabilization. They exist simultaneously. Therefore, don't say that stabilization comes first or vice versa. If you speak well but harbor evil thoughts inside, your stabilization and wisdom are not real. If your heart and speech are both good, inside and outside are one. Then your stabilization and wisdom are balanced.

"Stabilization and insightful wisdom are like a lamp and its light. Where there is a lamp, there is light; without a lamp, there is darkness. The lamp is the body of the light; the light is the function of the lamp. The names are two, but in reality they are one and the same. The relationship of stabilization and insightful wisdom is also like this."

Direct Mind is the Site of Enlightenment

The Sixth Patriarch said: "Total concentration on one single practice requires a focus and direct mind in all situations regardless what you are doing. *The Pure Name Sutra* says, "The direct mind is the site of enlightenment; the direct mind is also the Pure Land." Don't speak about directness when your mind is crooked. Don't speak about concentration on a single practice when your mind is not direct. Just act with a direct mind without attachment to anything.

"Confused people attach themselves to appearances. They cling to the idea that concentration on a single practice means sitting constantly without any thought. People with this view are no different from inanimate objects. This is the cause that obstructs the way. One should flow along the way without any attachments. If your mind fixates on anything, it is called self-constraint or bondage."

Freedom from Thought Fixation

The Sixth Patriarch said to the assembly, "Originally, the true teaching was neither sudden nor gradual. It is human aptitude that may be sharp or dull. Confused people cultivate gradually. Awakened people attain suddenly. When you know your original mind and see your original nature, then there is no difference. The terms of *sudden* and *gradual* are set up according to the difference of human aptitude.

"From ancient times, this school first established freedom from thought as the source, freedom from form as the substance, and freedom from fixation as the basis.

"Freedom from thought means being without thought in the midst of thoughts. Freedom from form means being separate from forms in the midst of forms. With regard to freedom from fixation, there are many human phenomena such as: good and bad, beauty and ugliness, intimacy and enmity, words and speech, offense and attack, deception and contention, etc. One should just see them all as empty, not be affected by them, or harbor any thoughts of retaliation. When all thoughts, past, present, and future go on uninterrupted, this is called bondage. When thought after thought does not dwell on things, then there is freedom without bondage. This is freedom from fixation.

"Outwardly separating from all forms and appearances is called freedom from forms. Being able to detach from all forms and appearances, reveals that the substance of all *dharmas* is pure. This is called freedom from forms.

"When the mind is not influenced by anything, this is called freedom from thought. Hence, the mind is always detached from everything. If one tries not to think of anything and eliminates all thoughts, when the last thought ceases, one will still be stuck in emptiness, and will sink into a deep void. Then one will still be reborn again, somewhere. This is not enlightenment. It is a great mistake.

"Thoughts are the source of all troubles. That is why this teaching establishes freedom from thoughts as the source."

Sitting Meditation

The Sixth Patriarch said: "In this school the teaching of sitting meditation (*ch'an*) has no obstacle or obstruction. When the mind is not stirred by anything good or bad in the external environment it is called sitting. Inwardly seeing the immutability of one's essential nature is called meditation.

"In terms of attachment to the mind, the mind is originally illusory. Knowing this, there is no attachment to speak about. Speaking about fixation of purity, the essential nature is originally pure. It is due to false thoughts that reality is obscured. Without false thoughts the essential nature itself is pure. Making an effort to fixate on purity creates the illusion of purity. In cultivating stillness, do not see people's good or bad qualities, rights or wrongs, faults or troubles. Then the essential nature will remain unmoved.

"What is meditative concentration? Outwardly detaching from appearances is meditation; inwardly freeing oneself from disturbances is concentration."

Repentance

The gentry and common people of the regions of Shao, Kuang, and the four quarters gathered in the mountains to listen to the Sixth Patriarch's teaching. The Sixth Patriarch took the high seat and said to the assembly: "With regard to liberation from the cycle of birth and death, it must come from one's own essential nature. At all times, thought to thought, purify your mind. Cultivate yourself, and work on yourself, see your own *dharma* body. See Buddha in your mind, liberate yourself, and discipline yourself. Only then will you not have come here in vain.

"You all have come from afar to attend this assembly because we have an affinity together. Now let us all kneel. First I will transmit the incense of the five-fold *dharma* body in your own essential nature. Then I will pass on to you the formless repentance."

The assembly knelt and the Sixth Patriarch said: "First is the incense of morality: in one's mind there is no wrong, no evil, no envy, no jealousy, no greed, no hatred, no anger. This is called the incense of morality.

"Second is the incense of stability: seeing all kinds of good and bad things without being disturbed in one's mind is called the incense of stability.

"Third is the incense of wisdom: having no obstruction in one's mind and constantly observing one's self-nature with discernment. This is called the incense of wisdom. Do not do anything bad. Even when one does good, one's mind should not get attached to it. Being respectful of elders and considerate of the young, while being sympathetic and compassionate to the orphaned and the poor. This is called the incense of wisdom.

"Fourth is the incense of liberation: when the mind does not fixate on anything, does not think of good or bad, it is free and unobstructed. This is called the incense of liberation.

"Fifth is the incense of liberated knowledge and vision: when the mind remains unattached to anything, good or bad, and refrains from sinking into the state of vacuity. This is the incense of liberated knowledge and vision. In addition, study broadly and learn a lot. Recognize one's original mind and penetrate the principles of Buddha's teaching. Maintain harmony with people. Do away with thoughts of self and others. Attain enlightenment directly. This is called the incense of liberated knowledge and vision.

"The five incense perfumes are inside of you. Don't seek them from outside. Now I will transmit the formless repentance to you to eliminate all sins of the past, present, and future, so that you can attain the purity of body, word, and thought."

The Sixth Patriarch explained: "Repentance means repenting all past mistakes, bad actions, and faults, such as stupidity, arrogance, delusion, jealousy, and deceit: repenting all of them so that they will never happen again. Repentance also means preventing future mistakes. From this moment on, be alert and do not commit any mistakes or bad behavior again. This is called repentance.

"However, ordinary people who are ignorant and confused only know how to repent their past mistakes and do not know how to stop from committing faults in the future. Because they do not repent their future faults, their past mistakes remain and future faults will arise. This cannot be considered repentance."

The Three Treasures

The Sixth Patriarch continued: "Now I will transmit the formless Three Treasures to you."

He urged the crowd to take refuge in the Three Treasures inside their own essential nature: "*Buddha* is awareness, *dharma* is truth, and *sangha* (the Buddhist community) is purity. Therefore, all things are inside your essential nature. It is like the sky, always clear, and the sun and the moon, always shining. When the sun is blocked by drifting clouds, above the clouds all remains bright, but below all is darkness. Suddenly a wind blows away the clouds. Then both above and below are bright and the myriad things appear.

"The nature of ordinary people is always unstable like the drifting clouds in the sky. Wisdom is like the sun and the moon, always bright and shining. When self-nature is obscured by scattered thoughts like the drifting clouds, one loses the clarity. If one meets an enlightened teacher and hears the true teaching, and can get rid of confusion by oneself, then one is completely clear, both inside and outside. Then all things appear within one's essential nature. People who see their essential nature are like that. This is called 'the Buddha of the pure *dharma* body.'"

Fa-hai

The monk Fa-hai of Ch'u-chiang asked the Sixth Patriarch in his first meeting, "Please explain to me how the mind (heart) is Buddha?"

The Sixth Patriarch replied: "When the first thought is produced, that is mind (heart) itself. When succeeding thoughts are not annihilated, that is Buddha. Producing all forms is mind. Separate from all forms is Buddha."

Then the Sixth Patriarch presented this verse:

"The mind is called wisdom.
The Buddha is stability.
Stability and wisdom are equal as one.
The mind is pure.
To understand this teaching,
Rely on your own habitual disposition.
It's application is originally without birth.
Cultivating both is the right way."

Fa-hai was greatly enlightened by these words. He responded with a verse of praise:

"The mind (heart) itself is originally Buddha.
Because of lack of understanding, we impede ourselves.
I know the source of stability and wisdom,
Cultivating both of them separate from all things."

Fa-ta

The monk Fa-ta was a native of Hung-chou. He joined the order at the age of seven and constantly recited *The Lotus Sutra*. One day when he bowed before the Sixth Patriarch, his head did not touch the ground.

The Sixth Patriarch scolded him, "If you bow without your head touching the ground, it is better that you not bow at all! You must have something in your mind that you're proud of."

Fa-ta replied, "I have recited *The Lotus Sutra* over 3,000 times!"

The Sixth Patriarch said: "If you had recited *The Lotus Sutra* 10,000 times and understood it's real meaning, then you could walk along with me. But now you are so overbearing, without proper courtesy and do not even recognize your own faults."

The Sixth Patriarch said, "Listen to my verse:

Originally, the courtesy of bowing was for cutting off arrogance.
Why don't you touch your head to the ground?
Ego leads to faults.
Forgetting merits brings endless blessings."

Then the Sixth Patriarch presented another verse:

"Your name Fa-ta means 'reaching the truth.'
Earnestly recite *The Lotus Sutra* without a pause.
Reciting by rote is useless.
One who sees his own mind is called a *bodhisattva*.
Since you have affinity with me,
I will explain it for you.
Just silently trust in Buddha,
And lotus flowers will bloom from your mouth."

Fa-ta apologized and said, "From now on I will be humble and respect all. I have been reciting *The Lotus Sutra* without understanding its meaning. I often have doubts in my mind. Your wisdom is vast. Please will you explain the principle of *The Lotus Sutra* for me?"

The Sixth Patriarch replied: "The principle of the *sutra* is very profound, but your mind is not. There is nothing doubtful in the *sutra*. The doubts are in your mind. Fa-ta, what is the basic principle of the *sutra*?"

Fa-ta said, "I am slow and dull. All I know is to recite the words of the *sutra*. How would I understand its principles?"

The Sixth Patriarch replied, "I cannot read. Please recite the *sutra* to me, and I'll explain it to you."

Fa-ta started to recite the *sutra* loudly. When he came to the "Analogies" chapter, the Sixth Patriarch said, "Stop!" Then he explained that the essence of the *sutra* is that the appearance of Buddhas in this world is for a great cause: namely the knowledge and vision of all Buddhas. People of the world are confused. Externally they dwell on appearances and internally they dwell on emptiness. If one can separate from appearances in the midst of appearances and free oneself from emptiness in the midst of emptiness, then the mind will open. This is the opening of the knowledge and vision of the Buddha.

The Sixth Patriarch clarified many points for Fa-ta, who wept with joy and gratitude and was greatly enlightened.

Biksu Chih-T'ung

Biksu (monk) Chih-T'ung was a native on An-feng. He had read *The Lankavatara Sutra* over a thousand times, but still he did not understand the meaning of "three bodies" and "four wisdoms." After making obeisance to the Sixth Patriarch, he asked for an explanation of the meaning.

The Sixth Patriarch said: "The pure *dharma* body, your essential nature; the fulfilled body of reward, your wisdom; the one hundred thousand myriad transformation bodies, your activity. If the three bodies are separated from original nature one has only bodies without wisdom. If one realizes that the three bodies have no separate self-nature, it is called the four wisdoms. Listen to my verse:

> Self-nature contains the three bodies.
> When awakened they become the four wisdoms.
> Without departing from what you see and what you hear,
> Transcend worldliness and ascend to Buddhahood."

Chih-T'ung asked, "May I also know the meaning of the four wisdoms?"

The Sixth Patriarch replied, "Since you understand the three bodies you should also understand the four wisdoms. If you separate the four wisdoms from the three bodies, you have wisdom without body, hence, wisdom becomes non-wisdom.

The perfect mirror like wisdom is pure by nature.
The equality wisdom frees the mind from all diseases.
The all-discerning wisdom sees all things without effort.
The all-accomplishing wisdom is as pure as the perfect mirror like wisdom."

Instantly Chih-T'ung realized the wisdom of the essential nature. Then he submitted a verse:

"Three bodies are my basic substance.
Four wisdoms are my bright original mind.
Bodies and wisdoms merge without obstruction
And act according to natural disposition.
Unnatural practice is the wrong way,
Rigidity is not the true spirit.
With the subtle theme elucidated by the Sixth Patriarch,
My confusion is gone."

Biksu Chih-Ch'ang

Biksu Chih-Ch'ang joined the order at an early age and was determined to see his essential nature. He had gone to White Peak Mountain to study under Master Ta-T'ung. One day he came to see the Sixth Patriarch who asked him, "Where are you from and what do you want?"

Biksu Chih-Ch'ang replied, "I come from White Peak Mountain where I tried to learn the principle of seeing my essential nature and realize Buddhahood from Master Ta-T'ung. However I have not resolved my doubts."

The Sixth Patriarch asked, "What instruction have you received from Master Ta-T'ung?"

Biksu Chih-Ch'ang replied, "I was there for three months and did not receive any instruction. Being anxious for the *dharma*, one night I went alone to the abbot's room and asked, 'What is my original mind and original nature?' Master Ta-T'ung replied, 'Do you see empty space? Do you see that space has any form?' I said, 'Space has no form, how can it have any appearance?' Master Ta-T'ung replied, 'Your original nature is like that. To understand that nothing can be seen is called real seeing; to know that nothing can be known is called real knowing. There is no blue or yellow, long or short. Just by seeing the purity of the original source and the complete luminosity is called realizing Buddhahood by seeing essential nature. It is also called the knowledge and vision of the *dharma* body.' However, I still do not understand it."

The Sixth Patriarch said: "This explanation still maintains the duality of seeing and knowing. That is why you do not understand. Listen to this verse:

Not seeing a single thing, yet still maintaining non-seeing
Is like floating clouds blocking the sun.
Not knowing a single thing, yet still holding onto empty knowing
Is like a flash of lightning in the sky.
How can original nature be seen?
Realize your error instantly,
And your own original light will appear."

Hearing this, *biksu* Chih-Ch'ang's mind was opened. He submitted this verse:

"Knowing and seeing arise without cause.
I sought enlightenment still attached to forms.
When one still retains a single thought of seeking realization,
How can one transcend previous illusions?
Self-nature is the original source of awakening.
By attaching to forms one will wander aimlessly.
Had I not entered the Sixth Patriarch's room, I would have been lost in duality."

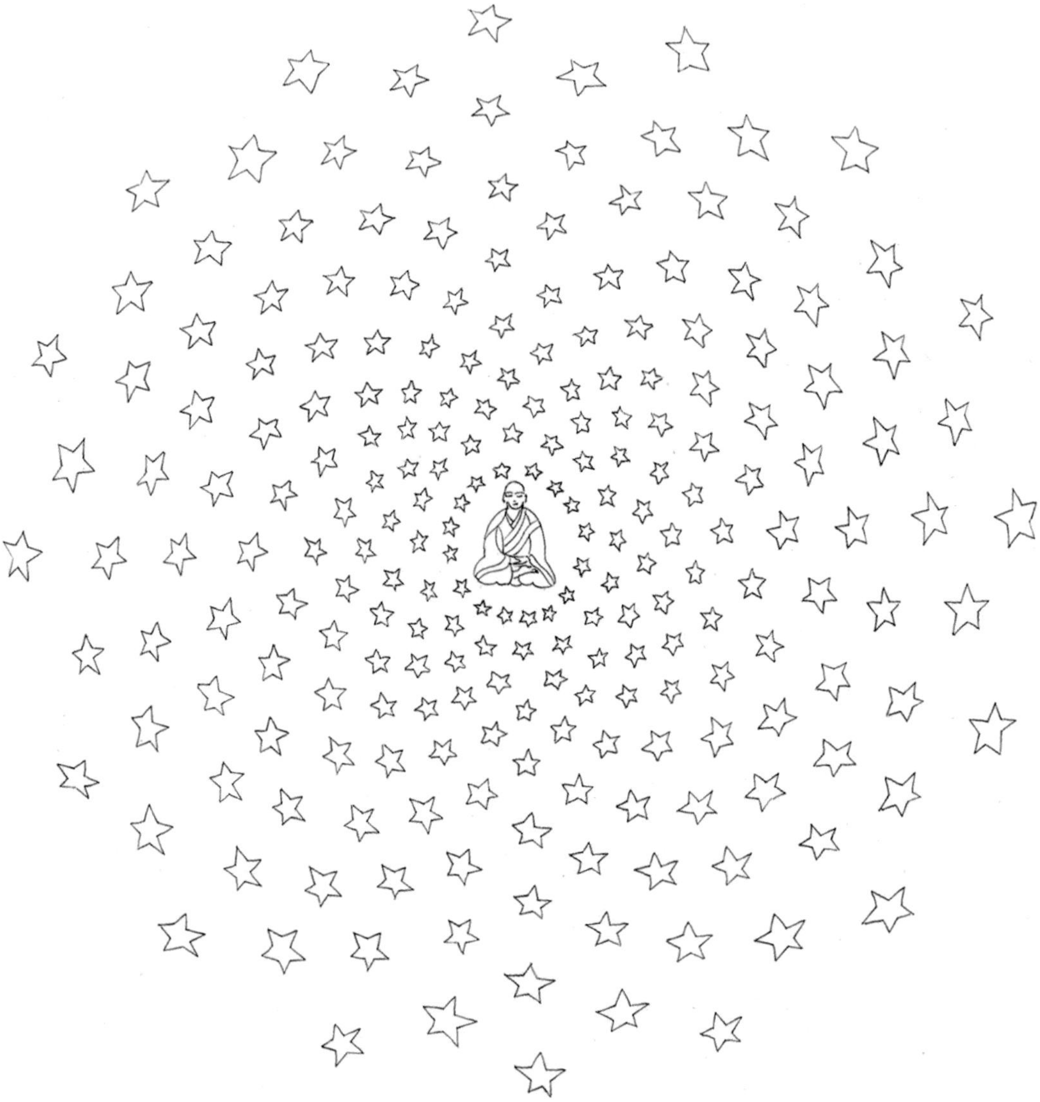

Biksu Chih-Ch'ang also asked the Sixth Patriarch to explain Buddha's teaching of the three vehicles and the supreme vehicle.

The Sixth Patriarch said: "Just observe your own original mind, and do not dwell on the appearance of things. There are no four vehicles, but human minds have different levels of intelligence. Vehicles are devices for practicing according to each individual's level. It is a subject for argument. Just cultivate on your own. At all times your own self-nature itself is 'Thus.'"

Biksu Chih-Tao

Biksu Chih-Tao, a native of Nan-Hai, Kwangtung Province, came to see the Sixth Patriarch for guidance. He said, "For more than ten years, since I joined the order, I have been reading *The Nirvana Sutra*, yet I still do not understand its deep meaning. Please instruct me."

The Sixth Patriarch asked, "Which part of the *sutra* don't you understand?"

Chih-Tao replied, "All activities are impermanent. They arise and then perish. When the cycle of arising and perishing is completed, quietude and extinction appear as bliss. I am confused by it."

The Sixth Patriarch asked, "How are you confused by it?"

Chih-Tao replied, "All living beings have two bodies, the physical body and the *dharma* body. The physical body is impermanent, subject to birth and death. The *dharma* body is permanent, but has no knowledge or consciousness. The *sutra* says, when the cycle of arising and perishing is completed, quietude and extinction appear as bliss. Then which body is quiet and extinct, and which body receives bliss? If it is the physical body, when it dies, the four elements disintegrate. There is only suffering, and suffering cannot be called bliss. If it is the *dharma* body which is extinguished, it would be like inanimate grass, trees, tiles, or stones. Then who is there to receive the bliss? Also, the *dharma* nature is the substance of birth and death. The five clusters are the function of birth and death. The substance has five functions. Birth and death are eternal. Birth is derived from the function of the substance. When death happens, the function returns to the substance. If rebirth continues, then all living beings would not become extinct. If rebirth is not allowed, all living beings would become extinct forever, just like inanimate things. Therefore, all things would be suppressed by *nirvana*. If birth is not allowed, how could there be any bliss?"

The Sixth Patriarch replied, "How can you use the outsider's dualistic view of annihilation and permanence to criticize the supreme *dharma*? According to what you just said, aside from the physical body there is a separate *dharma* body. You also said there is a body to enjoy the bliss of *nirvana*. This is clinging to life and death and indulging in worldly pleasures. There is neither the appearance of creation nor the disappearance of creation that can be traced. There is no birth and there is no death to be extinguished. Then quiescent extinction manifests. This manifestation is not measurable, and is called eternal bliss. This bliss has no one to receive it, nor does it have anyone who does not receive it."

The Sixth Patriarch said, "Listen to my verse:

The unsurpassed great *nirvana*
Always shines silently with perfect luminosity.
Ordinary people call it death,
Outsiders call it annihilation.
All these views are only mental calculations.
They become the source of the sixty-four wrong views,
Also the basis for establishing false names.
What is the real meaning?
Only people with supreme capacity
Are able to master the real meaning
Without grasping or rejecting it.
They know the characteristics of the five clusters
And the self within them.
They manifest outwardly all forms and sounds.
These are all equal, like illusions and dreams.
Do not hold onto the view of ordinary or holy,
Or regard it as an explanation of *nirvana*.
Cut off the three times and the two sides.
Use all sense organs as usual
Without thinking of using them.
Differentiate all *dharmas*
Without the idea of discrimination.
The *kalpa* (world cycle) fire burns the bottom of the sea.
The mighty wind knocks the mountains against each other.
Nirvana is true, eternal, quiet bliss.
This is the state of *nirvana*.
I am trying to help you renounce wrong views.
Do not take my words literally.
Then you may understand a little bit of it."

Hearing these words, *biksu* Chih-Tao was greatly enlightened. Overwhelmed with joy he made obeisance and withdrew.

Ch'an Master Hsing-Szu

Ch'an Master Hsing-Szu was born into the Liu family of Chi Chou. Hearing of the extraordinary teachings given by the Sixth Patriarch at Ts'ao-ch'i, he went directly to pay homage. He asked the Sixth Patriarch, "What should one do to attain ultimate enlightenment without sinking into mundane thinking of classes and stages?"

The Sixth Patriarch asked, "What have you practiced in the past?"

Ch'an Master Hsing-Szu replied, "I did not even think of the holy truth."

The Sixth Patriarch asked, "What class or stage are you in now?"

Ch'an Master Hsing-Szu replied, "Since I do not even think of the holy truth, what class or stage can I be in?"

The Sixth Patriarch was deeply impressed by his insight and high capacity, and asked him to be a teacher of the assembly.

One day the Sixth Patriarch told *Ch'an* Master Hsing-Szu, "You have a strong affinity with sentient beings. You should go to spread the teaching and do not let it die out. Having acquired the teachings of the Sixth Patriarch, *Ch'an* Master Hsing-Szu returned to Ch'ing-yuan Mountain in Ch'i Chou to spread the *dharma*. After his death he was given the posthumous title of "*Ch'an* Master of Universal Salvation."

Ch'an Master Huai-Jang

Ch'an Master Huai-Jang was a native of Chin Chou. He first visited the National Master An of Mount Sung. Then Master An sent him to Ts'ao-Ch'i to learn from the Sixth Patriarch. When he arrived and paid his homage, the Sixth Patriarch asked him, "Where have you come from?"

Ch'an Master Huai-Jang replied, "Mount Sung."

The Sixth Patriarch continued, "What thing is it and how does it come?"

Ch'an Master Huai-Jang replied, "To say that it is a thing is to miss the point."

The Sixth Patriarch asked, "Can it be cultivated and realized?"

Ch'an Master Huai-Jang said, "It can be cultivated and realized with a pure mind. But it does not work with attachment."

The Sixth Patriarch said: "Non-attachment is cherished by all Buddhas. You are like this and I am like this too. In India, Prajnatara predicted that a colt would emerge from under your feet and trample the people of the world to death. This means that one day you will have an extraordinary disciple by the name of Ma Ju, who will emerge to deliver many people of the world. Bear this in mind but do not speak of it too soon."

Ch'an Master Huai-Jang clearly understood. He attended the Sixth Patriarch for fifteen years and continued to penetrate into the most profound and mysterious *dharmas*. Later he went to Nan-Yueh where he promoted the *Ch'an* teaching. He was given the posthumous title of "The *Ch'an* Master of Great Insight."

Ch'an Master Hsuan-Chiao

Ch'an Master Hsuan-Chiao was the son of the Tai family of Wen Chou. In his youth he studied many *sutras* and *sastras*. He was particularly proficient in the "stop and observe" method of the Tien-tai school of Buddhism. Later, he realized the original mind after reading *The Vimalakirti Sutra.* One day he stopped to meet Hsuan-ts'e, a disciple of the Sixth Patriarch. During their deep discussion, Hsuan-ts'e noticed that *Ch'an* Master Hsuan-Chiao's words were in accordance with those of all the Grand Masters. Hsuan-ts'e asked, "From whom did you receive the teaching?"

Ch'an Master Hsuan-Chiao replied, "I heard many *Vaipulya Sutras* and *Sastras* from different teachers. Later, I realized the essence of Buddha after reading the *Vimalakirti Sutra*. But there is no one to confirm this for me."

Hsuan-t'se said, "Self-confirmation was permissible before the time of Bhisma Garjitashura Raja Buddha. After that, confirmation without a master belonged to the naturalistic schools."

Ch'an Master Hsuan-Chiao asked, "Will you confirm this for me?"

Hsuan-t'se replied, "My word does not carry weight. But the words of the Grand Master, the Sixth Patriarch are supreme. He is in Ts'ao-ch'i, where people gather together like clouds from the four quarters of the world to hear him. We can go there to ask him."

So they went to see the Sixth Patriarch. *Ch'an* Master Hsuan-Chiao circled the Sixth Patriarch three times, shook his ringed staff, and then stood in front of him.

The Sixth Patriarch said, "A *sramana* (monk) embraces 3,000 dignified manners and 8,000 refined behaviors. Sir, where do you come from to be so arrogant?"

Ch'an Master Hsuan-Chiao said, "Life and death is serious; impermanence comes quickly."

The Sixth Patriarch said, "Why do you not realize there is no birth and there is no speed?"

Ch'an Master Hsuan-Chiao said, "Once realizing there is no birth, speed no longer exists."

The Sixth Patriarch replied, "It is so. It is so."

Then *Ch'an* Master Hsuan-Chiao paid formal homage to the Sixth Patriarch with full courtesy. A short while later he was going to leave when the Sixth Patriarch suddenly asked, "Isn't your departure too speedy?"

Ch'an Master Hsuan-Chiao replied, "I am not in movement, how can there be speed?"

The Sixth Patriarch asked, "Who is the one who knows that he is not in movement?"

Ch'an Master Hsuan-Chiao replied, "You are the one making distinctions."

The Sixth Patriarch said, "You have realized the meaning of non-birth."

Ch'an Master Hsuan-Chiao asked, "How can non-birth have any meaning?"

The Sixth Patriarch said, "Without meaning, who makes distinctions?"

Ch'an Master Hsuan-Chiao replied, "Distinctions are also not an idea."

The Sixth Patriarch smiled and said, "Very good, indeed. Stay here one night."

Ch'an Master Hsuan-Chiao was called "The Overnight Enlightened One." Later, he wrote a very popular song called, "Song of Realizing the Way."

Ch'an Devotee Chih-huang

Chih-huang first studied under the Fifth Patriarch thinking that he had attained the true experience of meditation. He had practiced sitting meditation in a hermitage for more than twenty years. Hsuan-t'se, a disciple of the Sixth Patriarch, heard about him and paid him a visit. Hsuan-t'se asked, "What have you been doing here?'

Chih-huang replied, "Entering into stabilization."

Hsuan-t'se asked, "Do you enter into it mindfully or non-mindfully? If you enter into it non-mindfully, then all inanimate things such as grass, trees, tiles, and stones should have achieved stabilization. If you enter into it mindfully, then all animate beings should have achieved stabilization."

Chih-huang said, "I enter into stabilization neither mindfully nor non-mindfully."

Hsuan-t'se replied, "It is true stabilization if you enter into it without noticing whether you enter mindfully nor non-mindfully. However if there is entry and exit, then it is not the true great stabilization."

After a long pause, Chih-huang asked, "Who is your teacher?"

Hsuan-t'se replied, "My teacher is the Sixth Patriarch of Ts'ao-Ch'i."

Chih-huang asked, "According to your teacher, what is meditative stabilization?"

Hsuan-t'se said, "My teacher speaks of the state of meditative stabilization as perfectly serene tranquility, with substance functioning as it is. The five clusters are originally empty and the six sense objects are non-existent. There is no entry or exit. There is no stabilization or disturbance. The nature of meditation is not non-dwelling, separate from dwelling in meditative stillness. Meditation has no origination, nor does it have the notion of meditation. The mind is like space and yet without the idea of space."

Having heard this presentation, Chih-huang went directly to visit the Sixth Patriarch, and recounted his meeting with Hsuan-t'se to him. The Sixth Patriarch said: "It is truly as he said. Just let your mind be like space, without thinking of space; functioning as it is without obstruction; unmindful of action or non-action; forget the feelings of ordinary and holy; both subject and object will disappear; nature and form are as they are. Then at no time will you not be in the state of stabilization."

Chih-huang was greatly enlightened at these words.

Fang-pien

One day the Sixth Patriarch wanted to wash the robe which he had inherited. Since there was no good spring nearby, he walked a few miles into the mountains behind the monastery. There was a dense and lush forest permeated with good energy. The Sixth Patriarch struck his staff into the ground and instantly a spring appeared that swelled into a pond. Then the Sixth Patriarch knelt down on a rock and started to wash the robe.

Suddenly, a monk appeared and bowed before the Master and said, "I am Fang-pien, a native of Hsi Shu. Yesterday I met the Grand Master Bodhidharma in southern India. He told me to return to China quickly. He said that the true *dharma* of the mind's eye of Buddha and the robe he inherited from Mahakasyapa have been transmitted to the sixth generation in Ts'ao-Ch'i. Go to see him. Now I have come a long way. Please will you show me the robe and the bowl that you have inherited?"

After showing him the robe and bowl, the Sixth Patriarch asked, "What work do you do?"

Fang-pien said, "I am a good sculptor."

The Sixth Patriarch said, "Then please make a sculpture of me!"

Fang-pien was puzzled, but a few days later he completed a lifelike image of the Patriarch. It had fine details and was seven inches high. When he presented it to the Sixth Patriarch, the Patriarch laughed out loud and said, "You understand the nature of sculpting, but you do not understand the nature of Buddha." Then the Master stretched out his hand and patted Fang-pien on the head and said, "You will always be a field of blessing for humans and spirits."

Immediate and Gradual

At that time, while the Sixth Patriarch was staying at Jewel Forest monastery in Ts'ao-Ch'i, Master Shen Hsiu was at Jade Spring Monastery in Hsing-nan. Both of their schools flourished. People called them Hui Neng School of the south and Shen Hsiu School of the north. The two schools were divided into the immediate school of the south and the gradual school of the north, but people did not know the tenets of their teachings.

The Sixth Patriarch told his assembly, "The source of the teaching is originally one. But there are northerners and southerners; the teaching is one, but the comprehension of people may be quick or slow. What is meant by immediate and gradual? In reality the true *dharma* has nothing immediate or gradual. It is people who may be sharp or dull. Therefore the terms immediate and gradual were created."

However, the disciples of Master Shen Hsiu often ridiculed the southern Sixth Patriarch for being illiterate and questioned his merits. Master Shen Hsiu told his disciples, "The Sixth Patriarch has attained the wisdom that cannot be taught, and has profoundly realized the supreme vehicle. I am not his equal. Furthermore, my teacher, the Fifth Patriarch personally transmitted the teaching and the robe to him. How could that be done without good reason? Regrettably, I cannot make the long journey to learn from him, but you, my disciples, should not linger here any longer. Go to Ts'ao-Ch'i and find resolution."

One day Master Shen Hsiu told his disciple Chih-ch'eng, "You are intelligent and knowledgeable. You must go to Ts'ao-Ch'i for me and listen to the teaching. Try to memorize everything, and then return and tell me everything you've heard."

Following this instruction, Chih-ch'eng went to Ts'ao-Ch'i. He participated in the studies without saying where he had come from. Then one day the Sixth Patriarch told the assembly, "Right now there is someone hidden in this assembly that is stealing the teaching."

Chih-ch'eng came forward and made obeisance to the Sixth Patriarch. The Sixth Patriarch said, "You come from Jade Spring. You must be a spy."

Chih-ch'eng said, "Not so." The Sixth Patriarch asked, "Why not?"

Chih-ch'eng replied, "I was before I said so. Now I have said it is so, I am not."

The Sixth Patriarch asked, "How does your teacher teach people?"

Chih-ch'eng replied, "He teaches people to stop the mind, observe quietude in sitting meditation without lying down."

The Sixth Patriarch said, "Stopping the mind to observe quietude is not *Ch'an* (meditation). Sitting a long time constricts the body and has no benefit. Listen to my verse:

During life, sit not lie;
After death, lie not sit.
Still a set of stinking bones—
How can one attain the truth?"

Chih-ch'eng said, "I have studied the way under Master Shen Hsiu for nine years but did not attain enlightenment. Now hearing a single talk from you, I have immediately realized the original mind. The matter of life and death is momentous. Please be so compassionate as to instruct me further."

The Sixth Patriarch said, "I have heard that Master Shen Hsiu teaches the principles of discipline, stabilization, and wisdom. Please tell me how he teaches."

Chih-ch'eng replied, "Master Shen Hsiu says that 'not doing anything evil' is discipline, 'doing good' is wisdom, and 'purifying the mind' is stabilization. What theory do you teach?"

The Sixth Patriarch said: "If I said that I have a theory to teach people, I would be cheating you. I just untie people's knots according to their conditions. The principles of discipline, stabilization, and wisdom that your teacher teaches are very good, but I see them differently."

Chih-ch'eng asked, "But there is only one kind of discipline, stabilization, and wisdom. How can there be anything different?"

The Sixth Patriarch replied, "The discipline, stabilization, and wisdom that your teacher teaches are for the people of the great vehicle; mine are for the people of the supreme vehicle. What I teach is not separate from our own essential nature. Any teaching separate from the essential nature is called 'talk of forms.' Hence, it always causes confusion. We should know that all things come from the function of our self-nature. This is the true principle of discipline, stabilization, and wisdom. Listen to my verse:

The mind without fault is the discipline of self-nature.
The mind without stupidity is the stabilization of self-nature.
The mind without confusion is the wisdom of self-nature.
Self-nature is as indestructible as a diamond without increase or decrease.
Body goes, body comes,
With a pure mind,
It is the original *samadhi* (deep meditation)."

Hearing this verse, Chih-ch'eng apologized and presented a verse of his own:

"The five clusters form the illusory body,
How can illusion be the ultimate truth?
By trying to attain the ultimate truth,
The effort is not pure."

The Sixth Patriarch approved and said: "The teaching of discipline, stabilization, and wisdom of your teacher is good for people of lesser intelligence, while mine helps people with greater intelligence. If you realize your own self-nature, you do not need to establish *bodhi*, *nirvana*, or knowledge of liberation and vision. When one reaches the state where there is nothing to be attained, one is able to establish myriad *dharmas*. This is also called the body of Buddha and *bodhi* or *nirvana*, as well as knowledge of liberation and vision. People who see their own self-nature are free to establish them, or not to establish them. They come or go freely without stagnation or obstacle. They are able to act according to any circumstance and respond simultaneously when spoken to. Seeing all transformation bodies not separate from their own self-nature, thus they attain the freedom of spiritual powers and the *samadhi* of playfulness. This is called seeing self-nature."

Chih-ch'eng asked, "What is the meaning of not establishing anything?"

The Sixth Patriarch replied: "When the self-nature is free from faults, stupidity, and confusion, nothing is established. Observe all thoughts with *prajna* wisdom, detach from appearances, and be independent and free. Then what is there to establish? Your own nature is self-realized: It is immediate realization and immediate cultivation without a gradual process. What process is there? All things are nirvanic. This is why there is no need to establish anything."

Chih-ch'eng paid his respects to the Sixth Patriarch and volunteered to be his attendant.

Chih-Ch'e from Chiang-hsi

Biksu Chih-Ch'e was a native of Chiang-hsi. His secular name was Chang Hsing-shang. As a youth he had been a knight errant.

At that time the two schools were divided. Although the masters of both schools were not prejudiced, their disciples were competitive and harbored bad feelings towards one another. Secretly, the disciples of the northern school established Master Shen Hsiu as the Sixth Patriarch. They were jealous of the true Sixth Patriarch because he had inherited the *dharma* robe and bowl from the Fifth Patriarch, and it was well known. One night they hired Chang Hsing-shang to assassinate the true Sixth Patriarch.

Knowing the assassination plot well in advance through his telepathic power, the Sixth Patriarch put ten ounces of gold by his seat. That night Chang Hsing-shang entered the room of the Sixth Patriarch to carry out the assassination. The Sixth Patriarch stretched out his neck to the sword. Three times Chang Hsing-shang slashed the neck of the Sixth Patriarch, but failed to cause any wound at all.

Then the Sixth Patriarch said:

"A straight sword is not crooked.
A crooked sword is not straight.
I only owe you gold,
But I do not owe you my life."

Terrified, Chang Hsing-shang collapsed. He only came back to his senses after a very long time. Then he repented his crime, begged for pardon, and asked to become a monk. The Sixth Patriarch gave him the ten ounces of gold he was owed, and told him, "You should leave here now. I am afraid some of my disciples may do you harm. Change your appearance and come back some day and then I will accept you."

At this instruction Chiang Hsing-shang disappeared into the night. Later he became a monk and practiced vigorously. One day, remembering the words of the Sixth Patriarch, he made a long journey to see him.

The Sixth Patriarch said, "I have been thinking about you. What took you so long?"

Chiang Hsing-shang answered, "You forgave my crime before. But now that I am a monk I have no way to ever repay your kindness. I am wondering how I can spread the *dharma* and liberate people. I have often studied *The Nirvana Sutra*, but I don't understand the meaning of permanence and impermanence well enough. Would you be so kind to explain it to me?"

The Sixth Patriarch replied: "Impermanence is the Buddha-nature. Permanence is the mind discriminating between good and bad."

Chiang Hsing-shang said, "What you say contradicts the *sutra*."

The Sixth Patriarch replied, "I transmit the seal of Buddha-mind, how dare I contradict the *sutra*?"

Chiang Hsing-shang said, "The *sutra* says that the Buddha-nature is permanent, but you say it is impermanent. The *sutra* says that all things, good or bad, even the aspiration towards enlightenment, are all impermanent. These are the contradictions and confuse me even more."

The Sixth Patriarch said, "In the past, when I explained *The Nirvana Sutra* to the nun Wu-Chin-tsang, there was not a single word or a single principle that did not comply with the *sutra*. My explanation to you now is no different."

Chiang Hsing-shang said, "My comprehension is shallow and lacks wisdom. Please explain the *sutra* to me in greater depth."

The Sixth Patriarch said: "If Buddha-nature is in the state of static permanence, then it is senseless discussing good or bad things (*dharmas*). Not a single person would ever aspire towards enlightenment. That is why I say Buddha-nature is impermanent. This is exactly what Buddha meant by the true nature of permanence. Also, if all things are impermanent, it means everything has its own self-nature subject to birth and death. Then the nature of true permanence would not be pervasive. That is why I say it is permanent. This is exactly what Buddha meant by true impermanence. Because ordinary people and outsiders cling to static phenomena as permanence, people of the two vehicles also mistake the true reality for impermanence. In order to repudiate the wrong view of duality, Buddha clearly explained in *The Nirvana Sutra* the meaning of true permanence, true bliss, true self, and true purity. In reality, the Buddha-nature is neither permanent nor impermanent. If you only follow the words of the *sutra*, consider static phenomena as permanent and nihilistic phenomena as impermanent, you'll miss the true meaning of Buddha's subtle final statement. Even if you read the *sutra* 1,000 times you will not gain any benefit."

Chiang Hsing-shang was suddenly greatly enlightened, and presented this verse:

"Because the mind is attached to impermanence,
Buddha said that is the nature of permanence.
Those who do not know the right way,
Are like the blind underwater counting grains of sand.
Now without any effort of my own,
The Buddha-nature manifests.
It is not transmitted by the Master,
Nor have I gained anything."

The Sixth Patriarch said, "Now you have reached the truth. You should be named Chih-Ch'e, "one who understands completely.""

Shen-hui

A thirteen year old boy named Shen-hui came from Jade Spring to pay homage to the Sixth Patriarch.

The Master said, "My knowledgeable friend, you have come a long way. Have you seen your origin yet? If you have seen your origin, you should know the host. Will you try to explain it to me?"

Shen-hui replied, "Non-dwelling is the origin, seeing is the host."

The Sixth Patriarch said, "Your words are polished, but they are not your words."

Shen-hui asked, "When you meditate do you see or not see?"

The Sixth Patriarch hit him three times with his staff and said, "When I hit, are you pained or not pained?"

Shen-hui answered, "Both pained and not-pained."

Then he asked the Sixth Patriarch, "Do you see or do you not see?" The Sixth Patriarch said, "I both see and do not see."

Shen-hui asked, "What is both seeing and not seeing?"

The Sixth Patriarch said: "I always see my own faults, while I do not see the faults of others. That is why I both see and do not see. You say that you are both pained and not pained. However, if you are pained, then you are no different from an ordinary person, who gets angry and resentful. If you are not pained, then you are like wood and stone. What you just said about seeing and not seeing are two extremes. Being pained and not pained are the phenomena of arising and perishing. You don't even see your own essential nature. Don't use polished words with me!"

Shen-hui bowed and apologized. He thanked the Sixth Patriarch.

The Sixth Patriarch said: "If your mind is confused and you do not see, you should ask an enlightened teacher to show you the right path. If your mind is enlightened, you should cultivate according to the teaching. You are confused and do not even know your own mind. How dare you ask me if I see or do not see? I know my seeing self but it cannot substitute for your confusion. If you see yourself, you could not substitute for my confusion either."

Shen-hui bowed more than 100 times and asked forgiveness for his errors.

One day the Sixth Patriarch told the assembly, "I have one thing that has no head and no tail, no name, no label, no back or front. Do you know what it is?"

Shen-hui stepped forward and said, "This is the original source of all Buddhas and also Shen-hui's Buddha-nature."

The Sixth Patriarch said, "I just told you that it has no name or label. Immediately you label it and call it the original source of Buddha-nature. In the future, even when you start to preach the *dharma*, you will still remain as a monk with intellectual understanding."

Many years later, when the Sixth Patriarch had passed away, Shen-hui went to the capital where he promoted the teaching of immediacy of Ts'ao-Ch'i. He also wrote a very popular treatise called *The Revelation of the Source*.

There were many critics from other schools who gathered in the Master's assembly. They came with evil intent and ready to raise difficult questions. Pitying them, the Sixth Patriarch told them, "People who study the way should eliminate all thoughts of good or bad. What can't be named by any name is called self-nature. The nature without duality is called true nature. On the basis of true nature, all ways of teaching are established. If you understand these words, you should be able to see your self-nature immediately."

Hearing this, they all made obeisance and asked the Sixth Patriarch to be their Master.

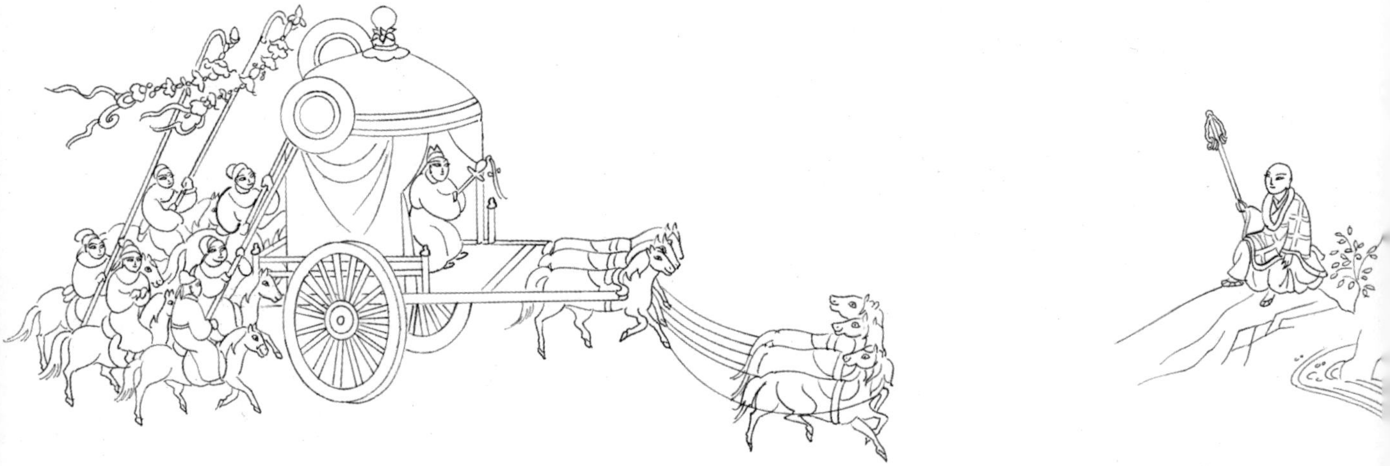

Imperial Invitation

On New Year's day of Shen-lung, 705 A.D., Emperor Chung-tsung and Empress Tse-t'ien extended an invitation to the Sixth Patriarch stating: "We invited Masters Hui-An and Shen Hsiu to court to receive our offering, so that we could study the great vehicle from them in our spare time after state duties. But both Masters very humbly deferred. They suggested that *Ch'an* Master Hui Neng come instead because the *dharma* and the robe had been transmitted to him from the Fifth Patriarch, as well as the seal of the Buddha-mind. He is the one who should be invited to court to answer all questions submitted to him. Now we are sending our court official Shieh Chien to deliver the invitation. We hope that the Sixth Patriarch will be so kind as to accept our invitation and quickly come to the capital."

The Sixth Patriarch declined the invitation on the grounds of illness and old age and expressed his wish to spend the rest of his days in the forest.

Shieh Chien said, "The practitioners of the way in the capital all say that if one wants to attain the way, one must practice meditation and stabilization. Nobody has ever attained liberation without practicing meditation and stabilization. Can you tell me what is the way that you teach?"

The Sixth Patriarch said: "The way is realized by the mind. It is not by sitting. *The Diamond Sutra* says, 'If you say the way of Buddha is sitting or lying down, you are on the wrong path. Why? Coming from nowhere and going nowhere,' without birth, without death, that is the pure meditation of Buddha. The emptiness and silence of all things is the pure foundation of the Buddha. Ultimate realization is without any concern for realization."

Shieh Chien said, "When I return to the capital, their majesties will surely question me. Would you be so kind as to explain to me the essentials of mind so that I can relay them to their majesties and to the cultivators of the way. For them it will be like one lamp, lighting a thousand lamps, illuminating the dark, lighting the light without end."

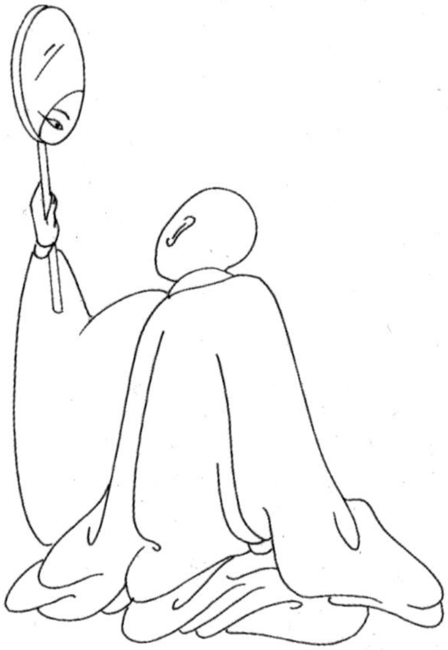

The Sixth Patriarch said, "The way has no light or dark. Light and dark is duality. Light upon light without end is finite because it is relative. *The Pure Name Sutra* says, 'Truth has no comparison, because it is absolute without relativity.'"

Shieh Chien asked, "Light symbolizes wisdom, dark symbolizes ignorance. If cultivators of the way do not use the light of wisdom to shine through ignorance, how can they depart from the cycle of endless birth and death?"

The Sixth Patriarch replied: "For the supreme vehicle, the truth has no duality. Therefore, ignorance is itself enlightenment. However, people of the two vehicles consider ignorance and enlightenment as two different things, but in the view of people of supreme capacity, ignorance and enlightenment are one. There is no duality. This is the truth."

Shieh Chien asked, "What is the supreme vehicle?"

The Sixth Patriarch replied: "Ordinary people see enlightenment and ignorance as two. People with supreme capacity realize that the essential nature has no duality. Essential nature without duality is the true nature. The true nature does not diminish in the ordinary or ignorant, nor does it increase in the wise and holy. It is not confused in ignorance. It is not quiescent in meditation. It is neither eternal nor non-eternal. It does not come or go. It is not in the middle, or inside or outside. It has no birth or death. It permanently exists and does not change. This is called the way."

Shieh Chien asked, "According to what you say about non-birth and non-death, how does it differ from the view of outsiders?"

The Sixth Patriarch said: "The view of outsiders regarding non-birth and non-death is that they use annihilation to stop birth, and try to use birth to express annihilation. It is duality. What the outsiders consider annihilation is not real annihilation, and what they call birth is not real birth. I say there is no birth or annihilation. That is the difference.

"If you want to know the essentials of mind just do not think of good or bad. Then you will naturally enter the pure substance of mind, always silent and serene, with subtle functions beyond the number of grains of sand in the Ganges River."

Receiving this instruction, Shieh Chien was greatly enlightened. After paying his respects to the Master, Shieh Chien returned to the capital to report the words of the Sixth Patriarch to the Emperor and Empress.

In the same year on the third day of the ninth month, an imperial edict of praise and gratitude was issued. It read: "The Sixth Patriarch has declined our invitation due to old age and illness. The Sixth Patriarch cultivates the way for us. He is truly the field of blessings for the nation. The Sixth Patriarch is like Vimalakirti, using illness to create an opportunity to expound the *dharma* of the great vehicle, and to transmit the mind of Buddhas as well as the *dharma* of non-duality.

"Shieh Chien has transmitted the teaching of Buddha's knowledge and vision which he received from the Sixth Patriarch. Through accumulated good deeds of our ancestors and good seeds planted in our past lives, we are able to meet the Sixth Patriarch at the time he appeared in the world and realized the highest vehicle. We are very grateful for the Master's blessings and we thank him profusely. Now we would like to present a fine robe and a crystal bowl to the Sixth Patriarch. We order the Magistrate of Shao Chou to renovate his monastery and convert the Master's former dwelling place into a temple named, 'The Temple of National Gratitude.'"

Final Instruction

One day the Sixth Patriarch summoned his disciples Fa-hai, Chih-ch'eng, Fa-ta, Shen-Hui, Chih-ch'ang, Chih-t'ung, Chih-ch'e, Chih-tao, Hsieh-chien and Fa-ju. The Sixth Patriarch said, "You are different from other people. After I pass away, each of you will be a teacher of a region. Now I will show you how to expound the teaching without losing the source.

"First bring up the three classes of *dharmas*, then use the thirty-six pairs of opposites to detach from both sides. When explaining everything, do not separate from self-nature. When people ask you questions, always answer with the opposite because opposites depend upon each other for existence, such as coming and going. Then both sides are eliminated, and nothing is left.

"The three classes are: clusters, channels, and spheres. The five clusters are matter, sensation, perception, condition, and consciousness. The twelve channels are the six external fields: form, sound, smell, taste, touch, thought, combined with the six internal sense organs: eyes, ears, nose, tongue, body, and mind. The eighteen spheres are the six fields of sense, the six organs of sense, and the six consciousnesses of sense.

"Our essential nature contains all *dharmas* and is called storage consciousness. When a thought arises it turns into consciousness. It produces the six consciousnesses which go out through the six sense organs and perceive the six sense objects. Thus, the functions of all eighteen channels are activated from our essential nature. If your essential nature is perverted, it produces eighteen kinds of perversion, as wrongly used by ordinary people. Essential nature is pure as it is. It produces the eighteen virtues. This is the way of Buddhas. Where does the function come from? It comes from our essential nature.

"In the external inanimate world, there are five pairs of opposites: heaven and earth, sun and moon, light and dark, yin and yang, and water and fire.

"In the language of *dharma* phenomena, there are twelve pairs of opposites: speech and *dharmas*, being and non-being, form and formlessness, matter and emptiness, visible and invisible, leakage and non-leakage, motion and stillness, purity and impurity, ordinary and holy, *sangha* and laity, old and young, and big and small.

"The function of our essential nature generates nineteen pairs of opposites: long and short, good and evil, ignorance and wisdom, stupidity and intelligence, chaos and stability, kindness and viciousness, morality and immorality, honesty and dishonesty, truth and falsehood, fairness and unfairness, affliction and enlightenment, permanence and impermanence, compassion and cruelty, joy and anger, generosity and stinginess, progress and regression, origination and destruction, the *dharma* body and the physical body, and the transformation body and the reward body.

"If you know how to properly use these thirty-six pairs of opposites, you will know that they connect all the teachings of all the *sutras*. Then you will be able to detach from both sides under any circumstances.

"When you talk to people, outwardly be detached from appearances, inwardly be detached from emptiness. If you fixate on appearances, you will produce false views; if you fixate on emptiness, you will increase ignorance.

"Do not fall into the state of thinking of nothingness. It will hinder your way and it won't help you reach enlightenment. By clinging to emptiness you will lose the middle way.

"If you only listen to the teachings without cultivating, that will lead to wrong views. Just cultivate according to the teachings and do not dwell on appearances.

"When people ask you about Buddha's teachings, if they ask you about non-being, answer with being; if they ask you about being, answer with non-being; if they ask you about the ordinary, answer with the holy; if they ask you about the holy, answer with the ordinary. These two ways mutually depend upon each other, creating the principle of the middle way. Follow the same way with all questions, then you won't lose the principle.

"If people ask you what is called darkness, answer that light is the cause, darkness is the condition. When light disappears there is darkness. Appearing and disappearing are mutually dependent, producing the meaning of the middle way. All other questions should be answered like this. In the future, when you transmit the teaching, follow this way. Do not lose the essence of the source."

Announcement of His Desire to Leave the World

On the first day of the seventh month of 713 A.D., the Sixth Patriarch gathered his disciples and said: "I wish to leave this world in the eighth month. Those of you with any doubts should ask me about them so that I can resolve them for you. After my departure there will be no one to teach you."

Hearing this Fa-hai and others wept. Shen-hui alone was unmoved and did not cry.

The Sixth Patriarch said: "Young Shen-hui has attained the state of equanimity: undisturbed by praise or slander, not thinking of good or bad, or sadness or happiness. None of the rest of you have attained this state. What have you been cultivating all these years in the mountains? What are you crying for? You cry because you do not know where I am going. I know where I am going. If I did not know where I am going, I would not have been able to tell you in advance that I am going! Remember, the original nature has no birth, no death, no coming, and no going."Now sit down and I'll offer a verse to you called, 'True and False Action and Stillness.'

Follow it and recite it, then you will be of the same mind as me. Cultivate accordingly and you will not lose the source.

There is no reality in things;
That is why we do not see reality.
If you see "reality,"
Your view is completely unreal.

If you want to know true reality,
Depart from falsehood; your essential mind is reality.
If your mind is not separate from falsehood
Where is the reality?

Animate beings are mobile,
Inanimate things are immobile.
If you cultivate immobility,
It will be the same as inanimate immobility.

If you seek the true state of immobility,
There is non-moving in mobility.
Not moving is non-moving.
Inanimate things cannot produce the seed of Buddhahood.

Be able to distinguish forms;
The ultimate reality is non-moving.
See it this way.
This is the application of the reality.

I declare to people who study the way:
Cultivate with a focused mind.
Those who cultivate the great vehicle
Don't cling to views of birth and death.

If you have a response from these words
Then let's discuss the meaning of Buddhahood together.
If you don't have a response,
Join your palms and be joyful.

There is no dispute in this school.
Disputes lose the sense of the way.
By clinging to your views
Your self-nature enters the cycle of birth and death."

Dharma and the Robe

Elder Fa-hai bowed and again asked, "After you enter *nirvana*, to whom will the robe and the teaching be transmitted?"

The Sixth Patriarch replied, "The lectures I have given up to now have been circulated and compiled in a book called, *The Altar Sutra of Dharma Treasure*. Preserve it, transmit it, and use it to deliver people.

"Now your roots of faith are pure and have ripened, and you are ready to undertake a great task. According to the meaning of the verse given by the First Patriarch Bodhidharma, the transmission of the robe is not to be passed on:

Bodhidharma's Verse
Originally I came to this land
To transmit the teaching for the salvation of confused sentient beings.
One flower will bloom into five petals,
The fruit ripen by itself."

The Sixth Patriarch continued: "All of you clear your minds and carefully listen to my explanation: Do not doubt that your self-nature is Buddha. Nothing external can be established. All things come from your self-nature; they rise and perish according to your self-nature. If you want to achieve wisdom you must attain *samadhi* of oneness of state, and *samadhi* of oneness of action. Detach from appearances, and do not love or hate those appearances. Do not grasp or reject. Do not think of loss or gain, success or failure. Just remain serene and empty, quiet and tranquil. This is called *samadhi* of oneness of state.

"Also, wherever you are and whatever you're doing, maintain a pure and straightforward mind. This is the key and inner altar of your nature, and this is the pure land. This is called the *samadhi* of oneness of action.

"If people achieve these two *samadhis*, it is like seeds that have been planted in the earth. They are nourished, grow, ripen, and bear fruit. My teaching is like a timely rain, nourishing the great earth. Your Buddha-nature is like the seed that will grow when moistened. Those who follow my teaching will certainly attain enlightenment. Those who cultivate my teaching will certainly attain wonderful results.

Listen to my verse:

The mind contains all seeds,
With universal rain they sprout.
Suddenly realize the blossoming heart,
And *bodhi* ripens by itself."

The Sixth Patriarch continued: "My teaching is non-dual, so is the mind. The way is pure without any forms. Be careful not to dwell in the stillness and emptiness of your mind. The mind is originally pure, without grasping or rejection. Each of you must work on your own according to circumstances."

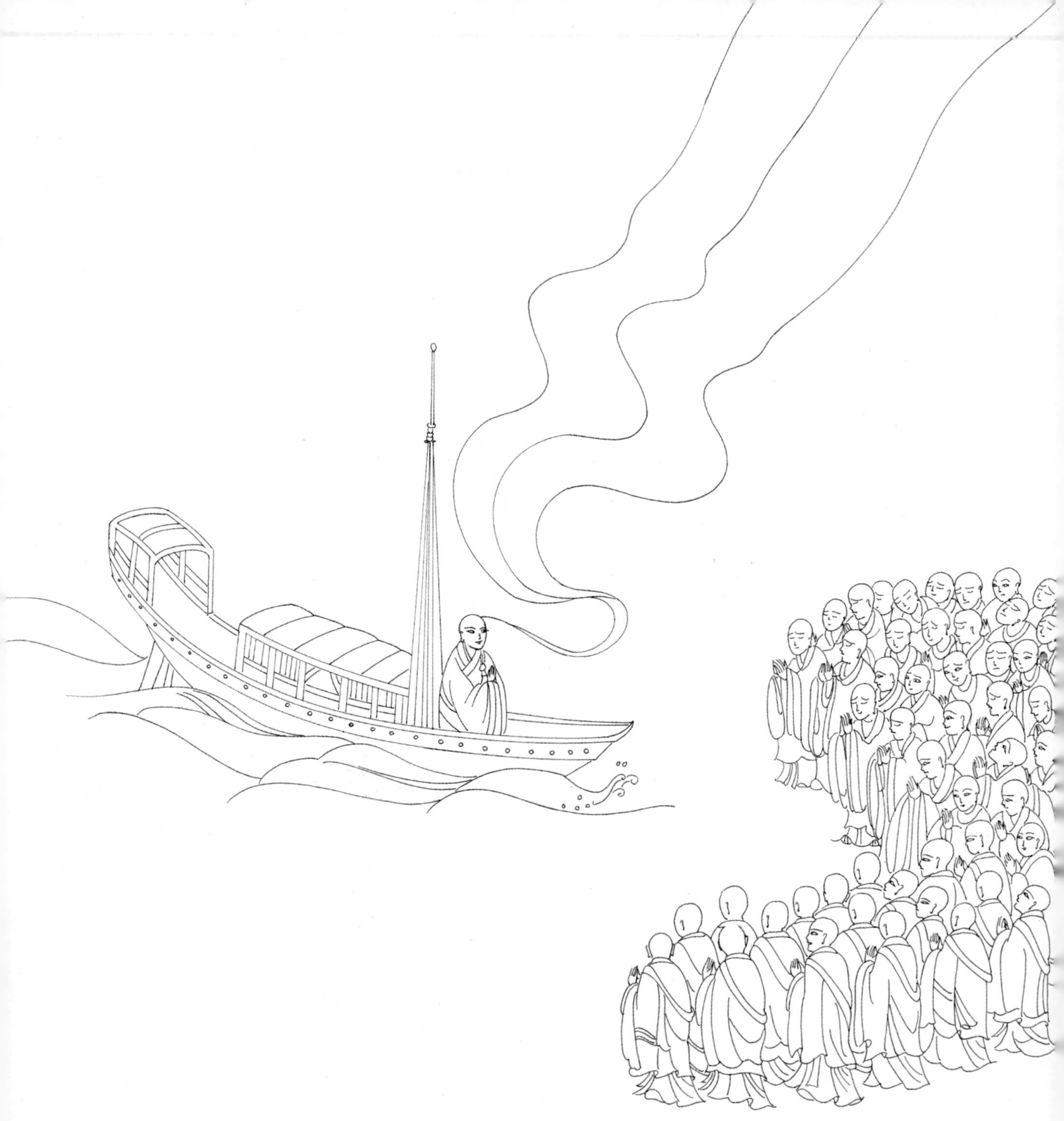

Nirvana

On the eighth day of the seventh month, the Sixth Patriarch suddenly told his disciples, "I wish to return to Hs'in Chou. Prepare a boat with oars quickly."

The whole assembly was saddened and begged him to stay.

The Sixth Patriarch said, "All Buddhas that appear in the world manifest passing away. Whatever comes must go. This is the eternal law. My physical body must also go."

The disciples asked, "After you leave, will you return?"

The Sixth Patriarch answered, "Falling leaves return to the root. There is no specific date of return."

The disciples asked, "To whom will the *dharma* eye of the treasure be transmitted?"

The Sixth Patriarch said, "Those who have the way receive it. Those who have no-mind penetrate it."

The disciples asked, "Please tell us, since the first Buddha appeared in the world, to how many generations has the teaching been transmitted?"

The Sixth Patriarch answered, "In the past the number of Buddhas that responded to the call of the world is innumerable. From Shakyamuni Buddha the teaching has been transmitted to thirty-two Grand Masters. I, Hui Neng, am the thirty-third Grand Master."

On the third day of the eighth month of 713 A.D., after a vegetarian meal at the Temple of National Gratitude, the Sixth Patriarch said, "Each of you take a seat. I am going to say goodbye."

Fa-hai asked, "Will you leave any more teachings to help confused people of future generations see the Buddha-nature?"

The Sixth Patriarch replied: "If confused people of future generations can see through the ordinary, they will see the extraordinary. That is Buddha-nature. If they cannot see through the ordinary, they will not find the Buddha-nature even if they try for ten thousand eons. When you know the ordinary within your own mind, you can see your own Buddha-nature. If you want to see Buddha, just see through the ordinary: When self-nature is awake, ordinary being is Buddha. When self-nature is confused, Buddha is ordinary being. When self-nature is impartial, ordinary being is Buddha. When self-nature is biased, Buddha is ordinary being. If your mind is devious, Buddha dwells within the ordinary being. Our minds have Buddha within them. The inner Buddha is the true Buddha. If the mind does not have its own Buddha, where can it find the true Buddha? Your mind is Buddha. Nothing external can be established. Self-nature is the source of all things."

The Hymn to the Real Buddha of Self-Nature

The Sixth Patriarch said: "Now I am going to leave you a farewell hymn, called 'The Hymn to the Real Buddha of Self-Nature.' People in the future who know the meaning of this hymn will see the original mind and attain Buddhahood:

True self-nature is the true Buddha.
Deviant views and the three poisons are the demon kings.
When deviant and confused, the demon is at home;
When righteous and true, Buddha is in the hall.
When deviant and confused, the three poisons arise in your nature.
Then the demon king comes to live in your home.
Righteousness and truth eliminate the three poisons from your mind,
Then the demon transforms into Buddha.
The *dharma* body, the reward body, and the transformation body—
These three bodies are originally one.
If you can see this within your own nature
This is the cause of attaining Buddhahood.
Originally the pure self-nature is derived from the transformation body.
The pure self-nature is always inside the transformation body.
The pure self-nature directs the transformation body to the right path.
It leads to complete fulfillment without end.
Desire is originally the cause of pure self-nature.
Elimination of desire is self-nature.
The moment you see your self-nature you will know the truth.
If you acquire the teaching of immediacy in this life
And suddenly awaken to your own self-nature,
Then you will see the World-Honored One.
If you cultivate Buddhahood,
But do not know where to find the truth,
Seek the truth within your own mind.
Truth is the cause of attaining Buddhahood.
If you try to find Buddhahood without seeing self-nature
You will remain a big fool.

The teaching of immediacy has been transmitted.
You must cultivate yourself before helping other people of the world.
I want to remind students of the way
If you do not see it this way, you will still remain far-away."

Having recited the verse, the Sixth Patriarch said: "All of you stay calm, and do not follow the worldly customs of weeping, accepting condolences, or wearing robes of mourning. This is the wrong way. If you do these things, you are not my disciples. Again, I want to remind you, just know your own original mind and see your own original nature, which has no motion or stillness, no birth or death, no coming or going, no right or wrong, and no dwelling or departing. After my passing, continue to cultivate in accordance with my teaching as if I were with you. If you violate my teaching, even if I were still in the world, it would be of no benefit. Now listen to my verse:

Not mindful of good or bad,
Joyous, silent, and serene,
Mind detached from all the senses:
Magnanimity."

The Sixth Patriarch sat up until midnight, then suddenly he said, "I am going," and passed away instantly. At that time, a subtle fragrance filled the room. A white rainbow touched the earth. The trees of the forest turned white, and the birds and animals cried in sorrow.

In the eleventh month of the year, officials from the three counties of Kwang, Shao, and Hsio competed to welcome and house the Sixth Patriarch's body. A decision was made to burn incense and pray, "Wherever the incense smoke goes, there will be the resting place for the body of the Sixth Patriarch."

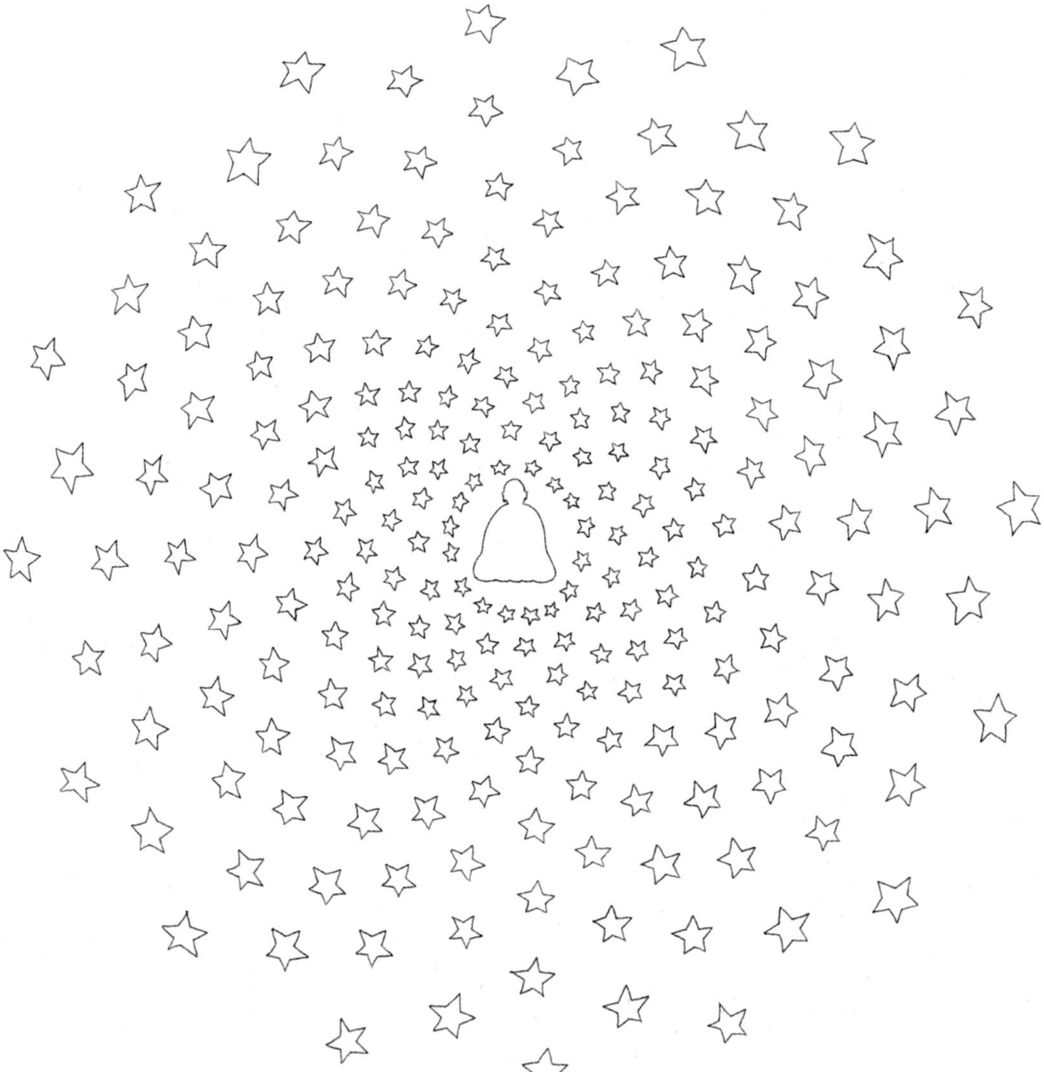

The incense smoke went straight to Ts'ao Ch'i, and so on the thirteenth day of the eleventh month, the casket, robe, and bowl were returned to Ts'ao Ch'i. Disciple Feng-pien coated the body of the Sixth Patriarch with incense paste, then put the body in a *stupa*. Suddenly a white light appeared from within the *stupa* and shot straight up to the sky where it stayed for three days. The Magistrate of Shao County reported this event to the Emperor. Then an imperial edict was issued, ordering the county to erect a stone tablet commemorating the life of the Sixth Patriarch.

The Sixth Patriarch lived for seventy-six years. He inherited the teaching, the robe, and the bowl at the age of twenty-four. He was initiated into the order at the age of thirty-nine, and taught for thirty-seven years. Disciples who received the essence of his teaching and became regional teachers numbered forty-three. The number of people who were awakened to the way and transcended the ordinary were innumerable. *The Altar Sutra of Dharma Treasure* has been preserved to this day.

Biographical Notes

Tze-si "Jesse" Huang is a professional translator and native Chinese. He was born in Chungking, China, the youngest of ten children. At a young age, Jesse stowed away on a freighter going to Hong Kong and Taiwan, where he stayed and prayed with the monks at various Buddhist temples. He eventually immigrated to the US, attending New York University and Columbia University for postgraduate studies. In 1975, he met his wife, the children's book author and illustrator, Demi. In the United States he worked as a financial analyst and manager in several US companies while continuing to pursue his love of translating from his native Chinese into English.

Demi is an award-winning children's book author and illustrator. She has published over 130 books during her career. Born in Cambridge, MA, she studied art at the Instituto Allende, Mexico; with Sister Corita at the Immaculate Heart College in Los Angeles; and was a Fulbright scholar at the Maharaja Sayajirao University of Baroda, India where she received her Master's degree.

Well known for her biographies of pivotal historical and spiritual figures such as Buddha, Krishna, Lao Tzu, Jesus, Mary, Muhammad, Rumi, Saint Francis, Gandhi, and the Dalai Lama, her book *The Empty Pot* was selected by former First Lady Barbara Bush in 1990 as one of the books to be read on the ABC Radio Network Program *Mrs. Bush's Story Time*, sponsored by the Children's Literacy Initiative.

In 1990, both Demi and Jesse represented the United States at the First Children's International Book Conference in Beijing.

Both Demi and Jesse are practicing Buddhists.

Other Titles on Buddhism by World Wisdom

The Buddha Eye: An Anthology of the Kyoto School and Its Contemporaries,
edited by Frederick Franck, 2004

A Buddhist Spectrum: Contributions to Buddhist-Christian Dialogue,
by Marco Pallis, 2003

The Essential Shinran: A Buddhist Path of True Entrusting,
edited Alfred Bloom, 2007

Foundations of Oriental Art & Symbolism,
by Titus Burckhardt, 2009

The Golden Age of Zen: Zen Masters of the T'ang Dynasty,
by John C.H. Wu, 2003

Honen the Buddhist Saint: Essential Writings and Official Biography,
edited by Joseph A. Fitzgerald, 2006

The Laughing Buddha of Tofukuji: The Life of Zen Master Keido Fukushima,
by Ishwar C. Harris, 2004

Living in Amida's Universal Vow: Essays in Shin Buddhism,
edited by Alfred Bloom, 2004

Messenger of the Heart: The Book of Angelus Silesius with Observations by the Ancient Zen Masters,
by Frederick Franck, 2005

Naturalness: A Classic of Shin Buddhism,
by Kenryo Kanamatsu, 2002

Sacred Art in East and West,
by Titus Burckhardt, 2001

Treasures of Buddhism,
by Frithjof Schuon, 1993

Uncompromising Truth for a Compromised World: Tibetan Buddhism and Today's World,
by Samdhong Rinpoche, 2006

The Way and the Mountain: Tibet, Buddhism, and Tradition,
by Marco Pallis, 2008

Zen Buddhism: A History, Volume 1: India and China,
by Heinrich Dumoulin, 2005

Zen Buddhism: A History, Volume 2: Japan,
by Heinrich Dumoulin, 2005